MARYLYN ABBOTT'S

thoughts on garden design

MARYLYN ABBOTT'S

thoughts on garden design

Kyle Cathie Limited

For Barbara Brandt Dalitz

First published in Great Britain in 2004 by
Kyle Cathie Limited
122 Arlington Road
London NW1 7HP
general.enquiries@kyle-cathie.com
www.kylecathie.com

ISBN 1 85626 488 2

Text © 2004 by Marylyn Abbott
See also copyright acknowledgements on page 192

Project editor Caroline Taggart
Design Paul Welti
Special photography Clay Perry & Simon Griffiths
Illustrations Katy Hepburn
Picture research Jess Walton
Copy editor Nicole Foster
Proofreader Penny Phillips
Index Alex Corrin
Production Sha Huxtable & Alice Holloway

Marylyn Abbott is hereby identified as the author of
this work in accordance with Section 77 of the
Copyright, Designs and Patents Act 1988.

A Cataloguing in Publication record for this title is
available from the British Library.

Printed & bound in Singapore by Tien-Wah Press

HALF-TITLE PAGE: *My beloved birch wood at
Kennerton Green (see pp. 13 & 87)*

TITLE PAGE: *The oriental vegetable garden at West
Green House (see p. 136)*

THIS PAGE: *One of my favourite 'steel' plants –
Eryngium maritimum (see p. 160)*

Contents

PART ONE

Thoughts on design & style 6

introduction 8

garden style 22

a garden's persona 40

garden rhythm 48

starting from scratch 58

a new garden – Scheherazade's paradise 66

decoration 80

PART TWO

Designing with plants 84

naturalising trees 86

shrubs 94

gardens with romantic themes 101

veiled glory 115

annuals 120

the cook's garden 130

designing with a single plant 145

designing with colour 160

garden design in the city 178

Index 190

Acknowledgements 192

thoughts on design & style

I believe I live a most fortunate life, totally submerged in tending (albeit with help) two gardens at the opposite ends of the globe.

It is now a decade since I made my first tentative efforts as a 'serious' gardener – a journey I commenced in mid life with incredible folly, for I stepped from creating wild fantasies in a happy-go-lucky weekender plot to making a new landscape around one of Australia's best-known gardens, Kennerton Green near Mittagong in New South Wales. Here, beside a

the Trust wished to sell on as a 99-year lease to someone who would restore the infrastructure and create new gardens.

Both the gardens are approximately the same size; both are, broadly speaking, cool-climate gardens, but with degrees of difference at the extremities of temperature. But both required new gardens in styles that were at either end of the design spectrum.

I think my story begins, as it did for many gardeners living in the 'new world', with the ancestors – the British

introduction

settler's enchanting white cottage, Sir Jock and Lady Pagan, two previous owners, had created an exquisite garden; but what had enticed me to the property was that beyond the small established confines were empty paddocks where I would be able to realise my own gardening ideas.

But, like Oliver Twist, I wanted more. I wanted an English garden, the inherited ideal that never quite leaves the colonist, even after five generations. I found it in the National Trust's West Green House in Hampshire, a small manor with 78 acres, ten of these a ruined garden that

colonists – alighting from the boat in the nineteenth century. Whether they had arrived at Boston, Cape Town or Sydney, they came from the hinterlands of British ports, perhaps London, Liverpool or Belfast, with visions of what they wished to achieve in their new homeland. The remnants of these ideas for house and garden still line mile upon mile of suburban streets and country towns on each continent.

It was the smallholder's dream: a cottage surrounded by a fenced garden, where all the desired plants of their childhood would grow. Roses were to cover the door, even if giraffes

were built not only in Australia but throughout the Empire, the remembered idea of an English country cottage.

nibbled the trees surrounding the home stoep in South Africa or if beyond the fence in Queensland, Australia, the cash crop was pineapples. The idealised cool temperate garden of the homelands was doggedly superimposed.

I have often mused on how much frustration would have been averted in Australia in the age of colonisation if the Spanish or another Mediterranean nation had reached here first, for their domestic culture was more adapted to an extreme climate. In Spain, house and garden were enclosed behind high walls that sheltered them from heat

and dust, and provided protection against cold prevailing winds. The precious water stored in courtyard tanks and ponds cooled the immediate air in summer, while the paved inner courtyards were softened by verdant pots and vine-covered arcades that filtered dappled light to the interior space.

But I digress. In fact, the colonists' desired English cottage design did not alter in essence for over a hundred years. In early Australia it was elaborated upon in larger gardens with collections of exotic trees, including the Bunya Bunya pine (*Araucaria bidwillii* 'Hook'), Norfolk Island pine (*A. heterophylla*) and monkey puzzle (*A. araucna*), which were added as affluence was achieved. But for most, a small patch of green lawn, using whatever grass would achieve this colour, sat at the front door. For my family, it was razor-sharp buffalo grass, *Stenotaphrium secundatum*, a coarse leaf that combated drought and was lethally uninviting for anybody wishing to sit on it. A straight path led from the gate to the front door, while regimented beds of European plants, edged with river stones or diagonally placed bricks, provided a gash of colour in a totally unshaded, dusty and laboriously raked yard. The overwhelming virgin forests were ruthlessly swept away, and it is only in

later colonial illustrations that trees reappear for homestead shelter, and shade verandas are attached to Georgian houses.

Of course, this view of gardening was not entirely static. This strange southern land had attracted botanists since its discovery, and botanic gardens in approved current European mode were established by civic authorities and aspiring colonists. In the early twentieth century, new gardening ideas were being acclaimed in England: the partnership of Sir Edwin Lutyens and Gertrude Jekyll, and the natural style of William Robinson were inspirations to a new generation. Edna Walling, a British-born but Australian-trained garden designer, became an Australian icon through her work, books and letters. In her popular magazine gardening columns especially, she brought these influences to southern Australian gardens. It was a more harmonious style, contouring the landscape with terracing and dry-stone walls, tucking in pools of water, and providing shade with vine-covered pergolas. Native and exotic plants were intermixed, and hard edges smudged with informal plantings. In fact, as a child I thought that all Edna Walling's gardens were covered with dusty cobwebs, just like Miss Havisham's bridal banquet, for she tucked *Erigeron karvinskianus* into crevices everywhere.

Growing wildly, its fine leaves, stems and daisy-shaped flowers caught every stray leaf and feather into its own ethereal growth, causing a misty effect over large portions of the design.

As a new gardener in Australia I did not even understand that my ideas for a perfect garden had been shaped by a cultural inheritance that was environmentally at odds with my homeland. I must pause here to tell you one of my favourite gardening stories. A short time ago, I was invited to South Africa to speak about the gardens and the techniques I'd observed whilst writing my previous book, *Gardens of Plenty: the art of the potager garden*. A good crowd of very bright gardeners had assembled in the Durban Botanic Gardens lecture room and I was in full cry, talking about how apple trees were espaliered around my potager in Australia, when at the back of the room a hand shot up and a delightful lady asked, 'I love espaliering fruit trees, but I'm in despair – how do I keep the monkeys from stealing everything?' I was really lost for words! Was this the perfect example of the problems of a superimposed culture?

I understood perfectly, as I had sympathised some months earlier with my New Orleans friends who were bemoaning the fate of a rose that was terminally distressed by humidity, loathing its conditions and hoping for a quick burial. And I have been equally foolish, insisting on growing a woodland of northern European white birch trees, *Betula* 'Moss's Variety', two hours' drive south of Sydney, defying the dry spells when a dozen or so trees perish each year – and all because my mother and I had dreamt of walking through a birch and bluebell wood!

It is still an unresolved dilemma, and as I've travelled and gardened in other lands I have seen many other gardeners gradually appreciating that their desired gardens are climatically impossible. For many of us, garden dreams blind us to reality and – however much we may want to fight good sense – in truth, our gardens, both in design and in planting, will not be successful until we learn to respect the climate and topography of our location.

We have to acknowledge what to expect seasonally before we conceive a design: when to expect rain and seasonal winds and what direction they come from; even the lengths and extremes of winter and summer. Some of our preconceived notions will probably have to be jettisoned straight away – such as the thought of a lavender hedge if the temperature is Nordic cold, or a rolling green lawn where the summer's length exceeds six months.

In my own gardens in the Southern Highlands of New South Wales, the winds howl in late winter – ferocious westerlies that would obliterate a garden if it were not ringed with windbreaks of closely planted trees and hedges. And the garden at West Green House is sited in a low cold pocket that desperately needs the warmth the old high walls provide. In both gardens, previous gardeners had acknowledged their climatic problems and erected screens to protect the design within.

Even in the same climate zones there are degrees of temperature difference. I started to plant *Iris germanica* in the UK exactly as I did at home, by placing the bulbs into the ground and covering them to protect them from the sun and obtain maximum moisture. Appalled, I watched a gardener in England come quickly behind me, unearthing them and planting them on top. Here, inches more rain and several additional degrees of cold necessitated a different approach to planting, although both gardens are classified as cool temperate. I thought I had taken the climate zone into consideration, but I had not truly understood the locality, and how plants should be treated.

The first country garden I designed for myself was grandiose – totally unsustainable, as there was not enough water or labour to maintain my vision. Moving to the city, chastened, I decided I could cope with a grouping of pots on a terrace. However, the sea at their feet and the marble terrace where they stood both reflected the burning sun, leaving my pots buffeted and defeated.

My next garden was on a sandy island swamp, which taught me the horrors of the greed, shade and continuous mess of over-large trees planted too close to garden beds. I still wanted to grow cool-climate plants, which was how, in the heady days of buying another garden, I exchanged one problem for another, for now I have an Australian garden that is always at the mercy of not enough water.

The potager at Kennerton Green, laid out over a decade ago, already expresses my delight in garden design with strict formality but exuberant planting.

I failed to see another design trap when I came to garden in England: the whole design structure was based on low clipped hedges of one plant variety, centuries-old *Buxus sempervirens* 'Suffruticosa'. Here is a warning for vigilance, a need for both care and knowledge when selecting the plants for such a design: when the bones of the garden are dominated by too many of one plant variety, it becomes very vulnerable. At this moment, an imported European fungal disease is ravaging many established gardens in England and I am seeing its tentacles decimate this design.

As I sit and write, the perfect example of a poor choice of design and planting material looks at me

across my dividing fence. Here, enthusiastic novice gardeners have planted over a hundred Leylandii cypresses – a rogue plant in shape, growth and looks – that will be an eternal problem for them and me, till they can be brave and take them out!

I tell these cautionary tales as parables, for these are some of the clues I wish had entered my head before I began to design my first garden. It is essential to have an understanding of the environment, climate and local vegetation; yes, even

the indigenous pests and creatures, for many of us are foreign actors working on an alien area of nature's stage, who will, by designing a garden, be superimposing our wills upon it.

Le Nôtre's gardens at Versailles, filled with fine objects and perfect linear design, have always enthralled me.

finding inspiration

A garden design, wherever it is conceived, will undoubtedly capture some of the soul of its locality from the sky, topography and surrounding architecture, so that the design is more than a plan of a series of paths, terraces or avenues. It is like a new birth that as it grows will gain some attributes and lose others, making a place for itself in the world.

I think most of us start with the overall concept, the plan of all the features – lawns, paths, walls, pergolas, pools and terraces – and where they will be placed. What is the style and is it appropriate? We think of the placement of major hedges, tree and shrub plantings and the flowering beds. Even when the future design is still just a matted clump of dormant perennial roots, it is in our mind's eye the perfect exhibit at the Chelsea Flower Show.

As a new gardener I found it was the overall garden design that enthralled me. I devoured information on historic gardens and designers. I soon began to assemble a gallery of heroes. Vanbrugh and Le Nôtre were superstars; Capability Brown and Repton were not. In the 1960s when I first saw Sissinghurst Castle in Kent,

I was spellbound by Harold Nicolson's plan but thought Vita Sackville-West's enthusiastic planting too gushing (oh, the arrogance of youth). Then I discovered Russell Page's designs, interspersing geometric water with green spaces and controlled planting. He became my ultimate hero – and he still is.

My inspiration is as old as gardening. Its roots are as much in Roman courtyards as in the grand parterres of Europe, with their great designs of green clipped box that looks as if it's embroidered on its white background. Russell Page's green linear masterpieces and the work of Arabella Lennox-Boyd are equally rooted in this tradition. Even the stark contemporary work of Martha Schwartz follows this precision. Often the plants are bit players within well-defined geometric designs, regardless of whether the garden is in the city or the country, a palace or suburbia, in locations as diversely placed as Nevada or Scandinavia.

My icons – Hazeley Court in Oxfordshire with its gigantic chequerboard topiaries originally conceived by Nancy Lancaster; Dr Carvallo's Château de Villandry, which boasts nine grids of vegetable gardens; or the highly romanticised work of English designer George Carter – do not stray from these origins.

For this exhibition garden at the Chelsea Flower Show, Arabella Lennox-Boyd has taken the rectangular shape of the display area and added linear style in the form of water, fountain, trees and stone to create a design that won 'Best in Show'. More importantly, by capturing light in a confined space and using a precise structure, she has produced a garden that is a year-round delight.

Nearly every garden presents snippets of inspiration. In Kew Gardens in London I noticed a patch of *Festuca glauca* 'Blaufuchs', which grows as tufts of brilliant blue and brown grass, begin to move. Mesmerised, I watched a flock of South African guinea fowl amble away, their spotted feathers in tune with the grass. Immediately my mind flashed back to the native stalls along the roads in Johannesburg where I'd seen local craftsmen's replicas of these birds. Nature had supplied inspiration for a small grass and sculpture garden.

As I walked through one of gardening's greatest achievements, La Mortola on the Italian Riviera, on a

ghastly hot day, the sight of a wall absolutely coated with the grey fur of prostrate rosemary was palpable aromatic texture that will, no doubt, appear in a future garden.

It is these shreds of stored memorabilia combined with lateral thinking that are the building blocks for design.

planting design

It took many years for my eyes to descend from the grand vision and to discover the joy of planting design. This is the detail of gardening, like the fine-tuning of an off-the-peg department-store dress to resemble a superb Valentino creation. I often enjoy playing couturier, to rearrange plants each season so that a new collection of designs can be

presented. Or, if I loved last year's achievement, it will remain and will not be traded in.

It is the infinite variety of shapes, textures and colour combinations that makes these small designs so alluring and annually fascinating to do. To redesign the hard landscaping of a garden, to create a wished-for new look, is often prohibitively expensive, but by a change of colour scheme or of planting – or perhaps just by the introduction of spiky shapes or clipped balls of different

The garden at Mapperton, Dorset, is framed by its own valley, with evergreen yew and box cut into important geometric shapes making a sympathetic hard landscape design. A tip for novice gardeners: the siting of the central pool is exactly correct. Water features always look better if they are positioned where water would naturally run – which in this case would be in the centre of the valley.

leaves – an instant transformation can be achieved.

I believe that a bold group of one species makes a more effective design statement, especially in a small area. I am currently besotted by the curry-coloured bark of *Myrtus apiculata*, a small South American tree with aromatic evergreen leaves. For a small town front garden, a group, perhaps of just three, of these wonderfully coloured trunks taking over all of the growing space, with sun spots of *Hypericum calycinum* colonising the ground beneath, would make a natural design that was also a privacy screen. Terracotta urns could blaze with *Achillea* 'Walther Funcke', the flat orange flowers fading to washed-out sienna, its grey lacy foliage a foil to the accompanying weeping strap leaves of *Hemerocallis* 'American Revolution', whose trumpets are blackened red in summer. Both plants are tolerant of dryness so are most suitable for pots, and their tones complement those of the trees.

I confess to being a dreamer, a perennial disciple of the 'what if?' and 'let's try' school of gardening, but now these fanciful flights are tempered by a little enforced wisdom, and the most divine ideas are slightly reviewed before I attempt to carry them out. I now know that the garden I desire must be one for all seasons, an

evergreen framework of plants; it may be embellished by seasonal planting, but these additional plants will be like an ornament on a dress – pretty but not essential. In these pages I have put together what is really a scrapbook of ideas that I have tried, with results that have pleased me. It is a collection of both the grandiose and the minutiae make a garden. It is a practical gardener's tale where every problem must be taken into account, even the most mundane consideration of whether the local pests – be they monkeys, deer, wombats, racoons, parrots, or even snails – make a design idea worth considering or achievable.

I realise I am stepping on quicksand here, for designs in art, architecture and gardening are a very personal choice, but by putting my mistakes, achievements and meditations together I hope I may give another gardener a few moments of contemplation and encouragement in which to convert their impossible dreams into 'do-able' reality.

Often we are frightened by the word 'style' because it is equated with fashion, the instant way-out chic of the catwalk, or with a particular period in art when style is a major statement of man's creativity. But just as in fashion or painting a designer's or artist's style evolves with the knowledge of his medium, so too our garden style will emerge with experience.

My journey began when I was a teenager and the only design that would have satisfied me would have had to rival Versailles. Next, I yearned

garden style

for a romantic garden in which every rose I planted had been immortalised by Redouté. But these visions suffered terminal shock when I heard garden designer Martha Schwartz at a conference in Melbourne describe her garden of purple bagels and a pool decorated by a grid of plastic green frogs. I thought her approach was simply marvellous.

I also had to ditch a childhood loathing for long grass where deadly snakes lurked as I sighed along with the wind in the great swathes of grasses designed by another American, James van Sweden. Then there were

LEFT & BELOW *Using all the elements of the Mogul tradition – narrow rills, brilliant tiles, water basins and fountains – in this desert courtyard, Martha Schwartz has created a modern American masterpiece whose inspiration is as old as time.*

OVERLEAF *With planes of rich colour echoing the colours of the desert's night sky, Martha Schwartz's hard landscaping and minimal use of native plants creates the sense of a garden in a harsh environment.*

MARYLYN ABBOTT'S THOUGHTS ON GARDEN DESIGN

LEFT *I am in awe of the drama that James van Sweden achieves in bold plantings of grasses in American gardens. Here, tall* Miscanthus sinensis *takes the place of traditional shrubs to frame a paved patio. To the bottom right of the picture,* Sedum 'Autumn Joy' *offers a splash of colour in a sea of golden and silver-grey textures.*

RIGHT *On the shores of Maryland, another planting of* Miscanthus sinensis, *growing over 2.5m (8ft) tall, catches every bayside breeze as it grows in natural partnership with a giant swathe of native prairie flowers.*

the clipped forms in all shades and textures of grey seen in so many dry gardens in Provence – a lesson in the use of native vegetation. These indelible impressions were absorbed over many years, and now I feel I have the confidence to analyse them and to identify the underlying principles that entranced me.

Firstly I believe that each of these gardens, whether large or small, was a designed stage set, where a collection of plants of definitive shape and numbers was arranged into groupings that gave a sense of occasion. To set the tone of the garden, each plant had a clearly defined role: perhaps trees and shrubs might be selected to create a soft and ethereal look with fine, filmy leaves and branches, while more rigid plants told a bolder tale. The square grid of clipped rosemary and lavender

balls in Provence was a dramatically grey-shaped picture against the indefinite grey landscape of southern France. Martha Schwartz's green frogs – again in regimented lines – told an immediate story of an emerald battalion, centre stage, surrounded by utilitarian buildings. A water-meadow garden in Dorset, designed by Arabella Lennox-Boyd and planted with floating grasses, fine willows and foam-flecked miscanthus, created a landscape that was so delicate it seemed to move with the sky, the movement framed by the most linear birch trees. In all these gardens, shape and texture have combined with colour to produce different atmospheres.

These gardens showed me that pattern needs a frame. I too like to encompass my garden design within the confines of a frame, preferably quite a solid and permanent one: perhaps a hedge or, if room permits, a good dense grouping of trees. And I like to be able to look down on the pattern, as on a carpet or rug, and see the complete view from the perspective above, even if it is just from a step or two, or a descending path.

The plants within my frame are very important, as they set the mood – but so too does the surround. Just as a heavy frame makes an old painting more severe, so the wrong choice of framing plant will not enhance the

LEFT *Tucked away in a hillside village in Provence, the late Nicole de Vesian created a series of enclosed terraces and planted them with the flora native to this hard terrain. With every shade of grey-green that looks like living masonry, this is perhaps the garden that has had the most influence on my precepts of garden design.*

ABOVE *Tightly clipped balls of lavender and columnar cypresses create strong form in front of a frame of Provençal countryside.*

composition within. In an urban garden, space is generally limited and a dark surround will optically foreshorten it, so in a confined space I like the lighter effect of the charmingly described 'tapestry hedge' – a line of mixed hedging materials that may include holly, evergreen viburnum, yew and some varieties of *Cupressus* to provide a subtle variation of green tones and textures. Clipped yearly, they will thrive whether planted out or arranged in tubs, lightly enclosing the design within. These are plants for all seasons: a cool line on hot days; a green wall when the world is grey or white.

Today many of us live within urban spaces, and the lives of other people encroach into our particular world. A hedge, whether planted with a single variety or as a tapestry hedge; trees that are pleached – a craft that is sometimes known as creating a hedge on legs – then perhaps espaliered, where all major branches are trained along wire

to make a wall; all will create a sense of privacy. Even where deciduous hornbeam, lime or beech has been used for height, when pleached or espaliered the branches provide an aura of privacy and security and can help to buffer an offending view.

I have suggested trees in rich greens, but the green grey is quietly harmonious too. I like *Sorbus aria* 'Lutescens' or *Acer negundo* 'Flamingo', which gives the impression of a near-white wall. The red- and burgundy-toned trees and shrubs, even the majestic copper beech, *Fagus sylvatica* 'Purpurea', I find strident and unrestful when massed. This is simply a personal view, though – a distinguished designer at a recent major garden show created an arresting landscape design in these colours combined just with grey. For me, its ambience was depressing and funereal.

Inevitably the planted frame will form a geometric shape – oblong,

square, semicircle or triangle – and into this space I wish my design to capture centre stage. To do this it must reflect light from the sky at all seasons. Shiny surfaces of polished leaves and flowers – perhaps buxus or camellia, to give but two examples – or the hard finishes of glazed ceramic pots and tiles, polished steel or glass are all light-reflective; brilliant hues capture light, while clear water is pure light.

I need my design to enrapture me all year, so permanently shaped plants in solid evergreens, others as branched tracery, and objects – perhaps sculptures, fountains, ponds or urns – will be used to support my growing composition.

Since ancient times, gardeners have made garden pictures from small-leafed plants cut out or trained into permanent shapes. Topiary is a superb craft for the patient gardener, but nurseries now supply tall spirals, pyramids, balls and multiple pompons made from, among many, *Buxus*

ABOVE & LEFT *Pleaching a tree can bring living sculpture to a garden. Just about any variety can be trained and clipped to form a line of pleaching, or a single tree can form an individual block. Here, deciduous trees are backed by an evergreen yew hedge which enhances the beauty of the shaped tree at this time of year, and will continue to do so once the leaves have gone.*

I believe that trees used this way bring not only height but great drama to a garden. Traditionally, limes and hornbeams are used, but many dense native trees would respond to this architectural treatment.

sempervirens, *Lonicera nitida, Taxus* and *Cupressus* varieties to place in the ground or to decorate pots. Even traditional flowering shrubs are trained to echo these shapes. Hydrangeas, potentillas and *Eucalyptus gunnii* – again just a few from an endless list – form patterns of their own in high season.

I believe extremes succeed – excess or minimalism. In my enclosed space I'd adore the fun of a forest of evergreen shapes, perhaps just clipped circles or cones, say seven if the space were tiny, though up to 30 is possible in a space 6m (20ft) square.

A similar effect could be achieved by a grouping of painted wood or steel tripods in exactly the same design but with varied heights. I'd cover them with the seasonal edible delights of beans, choco (in warmer climates),

courgettes and cucumbers, their feet in a rosette of lettuce or crimped paddles of chard. After harvest, the triangular silhouettes of the tripods would present pleasing form on their own. Or my seasonal plants could be flowers – inevitably roses and clematis, for a more permanent and luxuriant choice, while brilliant sweet peas with a sunflower trained in their centre could look quite dashing for a few weeks.

Or the focus could be just one cloud tree, made from a selected evergreen with its branches trimmed except for a rounded shape of leaves at its extremities. Balanced by a mat of ground cover at its feet, this one living sculpture makes a garden masterpiece on its own. But the size of the tree must be relevant to the area – a 1.5m (5ft) tree would look lost in a 9m (30ft) square garden.

The above examples are only one expression of style, using the soft landscaping of trees, shrubs and shapes which I prefer, probably assembled in a chessboard or linear pattern.

When I was a young gardener my mind dashed over many design spectrums until I realised all my passions shared a style similarity: I always liked geometric, regular design. Once I would have approached my garden plan looking into the garden from outside; I wanted to make the grand vista. But now my perspectives

ABOVE *Using growing lengths, a lattice pyramid is good architecture whether as a skeleton or covered with leaves. Using pliable willow, these living sculptures can be formed in innumerable styles.*

LEFT *For me there is nothing more satisfying than objects made from crisply clipped green plants. Here a traditional material has been used — yew shaped as tall, slim cones, in sharp contrast to the immaculate white gravel from which they rise. The deep green of the yew's small, dense, evergreen, needle-like leaf is a strong textural statement against the lighter deciduous trees beyond.*

RIGHT *Simultaneously elegant and fanciful, a mature example of a clipped box plant.*

FAR RIGHT *The effect of this smart line of clipped box balls could be produced instantly, for shapes like these are easily purchased. The rounded shapes provide defining symmetry for the already symmetrical beds on either side.*

LEFT *This small parterre of simple green lines makes an all-season picture in the heart of the garden at Kennerton Green. Made from clipped* Buxus sempervirens, *it is framed by mature plantings of deciduous trees and espaliered Granny Smith apples.*

have changed and I look outwards from the space I inhabit to paint garden pictures that inspire the opening of a window or the desire to venture outside. I want my garden to be a series of vignettes that lead from one episode to another, progressively unfolding a personal essay, often using just one style and texture of plant.

This is my preferred approach to garden style, but somehow I have to make my preference fit into the landscape I am in. I have to choose plants that are climatically practical, using colours and textures that are compatible, and arranging them to create great beauty and harmony.

I often wonder if new gardeners are too intimidated to find individuality, subjected as we all are to endless media advice so positively presented. Do we accept without question what the media say, conveniently forgetting that they scour the world for a good story? Television programmes, magazines and syndicated columns are sold internationally, so gardeners from Rotorua to Oslo will be presented with the same advice. Or are we so used to seeing stories and pictures from the world's beautiful gardens that we casually accept them and their local style, forgetting that it has taken generations to perfect the gardens' suitability for their environment? Too often we assume that this magnificence can happily be transplanted to anywhere we want it.

To proclaim a preference takes great courage, especially when we are surrounded by a phalanx of garden glitterati. I'm terrified by the 30-something male designers, particularly those who proclaim that old gardens like mine, whose bones are part of a gardening heritage, are dinosaurs. The new generation is introducing us to another concept, full of striking shapes and stiff, sharp and phallic plants; amok with hard landscaping, dazzlingly complex levels and surfaces, and computer-controlled water. The issue is raised of whether, in the confines of a modern lifestyle, hard landscaping is more important in a garden than plants.

This is a totally different view of style. It can be superimposed on any

landscape, for it relies principally on structure. It is often exhilarating and spectacular, so perhaps it is gardening's equivalent of the glass and steel office block, a global design, impervious to climate, environment and local tradition. But this is not for me – I still hark back to 'razored hedgerows, flowers, those planted trees whose avenues conduct a greater ease…', as Douglas Dunn wrote in 1789.

But time modifies all opinions. I remember the post-war European immigrants to Australia adorning their first homes with wide trellises of grapes, their yards becoming a network of beds where aubergines, broad beans and tomatoes appeared among the roses. We of the Anglo-Saxon tradition looked on in amazement, but these new gardens were in both style and plant material more in tune with our warmer climate that our English-inspired flower beds and lawns. These gardeners were able to sit out in summer under the cool vines, enjoying their produce and the pleasures of their creativity, while we viewed our gardens from behind lace curtains or from verandas covered with hot tin. Today such Mediterranean-style courtyards are an accepted part of many Australian garden designs, but they are often conceived for their decorative ornamentation; the essential cooling principles for summer enjoyment are still not understood.

Coming to terms with gardening in this, the driest continent, has been slow, and as climates change globally it is a problem that will affect everyone. Wherever we live we must design a garden that not only gives beauty and pleasure, but also is respectful of our natural resources.

I think we are on the edge of a new and extraordinary journey where we must be in tune with our earth, rather than superimposing our desires. We will have to re-evaluate every aspect of design, even the decision as to which colours will look fresh against a warming sky.

We also now have choices of plants in colours and textures not imagined a decade ago. Such choices, too, will be challenging, for although the plants exist, they need to be searched for. The majority are grown for mass marketing, and the accountants' requirement for instantly saleable products means that every plant centre on every continent is almost the same.

Gardening has always been polyglot in its ideas. For centuries the Mediterranean classical landscape provided northern Europe with its desired garden design. Then in the eighteenth century, botanists stepping ashore in exotic locations secured for their employers crates of plant curiosities, sending them home with the DIY instructions of the age. Often there were tantalising illustrations of Eastern architecture surrounding the new plants, inspiring the Home Counties gentleman to build temples,

economics dictate. Most of us will establish many gardens throughout our lives, in varied accommodation, from college digs – where a treasured pot on a windowsill is the only garden – to the suburbs or isolated farms, perhaps on the other side of the world.

As we move, carrying design experience gathered from layers of assorted inspiration, we could be called environmental terrorists, superimposing our preconceived ideas on the landscape where we settle. Is this the epoch when 'gardens of the mind' can

The eighteenth-century botanist could have used an illustration of the Emperor Yang-Ti (581–618) with his wives in his pleasure garden to show his employer how the blossom

a garden's persona

pagodas and enchanting Japanese teahouses. He combined whatever plants he pleased, splashing across the landscape his own concept of a perfect garden. It was an activity of a time that rejoiced in the new, created by isolated pockets of privilege, the fruits of which are still enjoyed after many generations.

But perhaps this is the dilemma, for that world has vanished and we exist in a time of immediate change. Very few of us expect to plant the proverbial acorn and watch it grow; we realise that jobs are not for life and that packing up and moving on happens as

be transferred to any place we choose to call home? I'm sure it is, and I think perhaps it's time for us to step off the carousel and become acquainted with the place and time we are in, to find the persona of our local environment, endeavouring to capture its spirit, so that perhaps we can design a garden that is in harmony with its location.

Of course we all wish for the dream garden, where the mercury rises no higher than 25°C and we are surrounded by verdant grass and flowers suffused with scent and colour, but any garden design is doomed to fail unless the vagaries of our

trees were displayed in their country of origin. It was from pictures like this that the inspiration for many grand English gardens was conceived.

immediate environment are understood.

The clues are already in place. The palm trees on a hot afternoon in the Moroccan desert cast bars of purple light on to the sandy earth below and, nearby, sharp patterned shadows filtering through grilles – some as straight as a palm, others like twining vines – made light designs on the enclosed courtyards. Surely these trees, and perhaps also these light patterns, were the inspiration for the tracery designs in Persian carpets or the abstract tile designs that pave hard surfaces. So just as the peoples of North Africa took their vegetation and light as inspiration, introducing native palms and hillside plants into these exquisite courtyards, so can we use indigenous plants of unusual form to cast unique shade patterns, and harness the tones of shadows, soil and native vegetation as the basis for colour design.

The local vegetation is the region's botanical dictionary and an inspiration for the choices of plants and colour. Dan Hinkley, the extraordinary American plantsman, has used the dark green forests of Washington State as foils for the boldest combinations of leaf shapes and colour. I wonder if a collection of these plants would look too strident against the light green of a northern European birch wood?

The grey greens of Provence or the blue-grey haze of Australia offer muted tones, and many of those regions' greyish, rough-textured plants absorb the excessive light. Grey gardens are very fashionable in cool temperate lands, but look closely, for the low light of these countries makes many of these plants look rather drab. Perhaps they need their home environment's tough light to surround them. Maybe away from this light they lose some of their personality.

Tropical trees and vines have a gleam of green neon light in their own habitat after their daily tropical shower, a polish they never achieve in other climates, just as grasses grown in standard clumps in European gardens never quite capture the movement inherent in native grasslands. The plant's persona tells us where it will look superb.

The colour wash of a landscape is also in its soils, be they delta black, red earth, white sand, gravel or any tone in between. Colours come from rocks, and the salts and minerals in the water. All these elements will also have a primary influence on how the garden picture should emerge. In many parts of the USA and Australia the stridently coloured soil forms red dustcoats on plants when dry, then stains the plants and buildings alike after rains. So why would we want to plant a collection of delicately shaded pastel perennials on it

in traditional European mode? Likewise the gravelly white soils of Provence seem to add a ring of light colour to the scrubby grey garrique, the native bush, giving it a reflected highlight that it would not get on loam.

Then add man's contribution, for these natural materials will colour the local buildings, supplying lime for whitewash or clay for render in tones of sienna. Red soils provide the materials for red brick and tile, as stony lands supply grey granite walls and slate roofs, with paving in flint, cobbles and stone. In the red-walled suburbs of Sydney, I fantasise about covering that aggressive colour with only champagne-coloured flowers – anything to soften its harshness.

For many years I did not come to terms with this in my native habitat, barely tolerating the climate and perceiving only the drab colours of monotonous bush. But on a warm November afternoon the family of the garden designer Michael Cook gave me a bunch of Australian wild flowers native to the north coast beyond Sydney. Extraordinarily coloured blooms in wild and weird shapes, they performed what a Billy Graham crusade liked to achieve – instant conversion. The flowers encapsulated the spirit of the land, so secretive that it is sometimes hard to find, presenting a different beauty, one that I should

have acknowledged and pursued before contemplating any garden design here.

And this could be said to be the crux of the matter for many new gardeners, and that included me. We looked at books and magazines with lavish photographs of superb gardens made with plants collected indiscriminately from around the world. They were so extraordinarily vivid they blinded the eye to the native palette. Perhaps it is like dazzling a child's eye with a cake topped with multicoloured hundred and thousands, so distracting them that they do not even consider the duller mounds of more delicious chocolate alongside.

As I travelled through the USA I felt that the presence of the land was

winning through. Led by garden designers who have taken their inspiration from the rolling swathes of native flowers and grasses, a garden style has been introduced that seems unique to America, its design inspiration based on the native vegetation.

Urbanisation has presented us with another habitat. It is of man-made colour, its sky often saturated with polluted air that coats and eventually kills vegetation. Unfortunately many of us live in this 24-hour world, where drabness colours our days and virulent hoardings our nights, but this again is all part of the local personality within which we may have to plan a garden. Recognition and adaptation must be our creed, to create harmonious beauty and a design to complement the immediate surroundings.

In the inhospitable conditions of the city streetscape, where light is low and diffused in canyons of deep shadow, perhaps we should abandon the idea of growing flowers and treat the garden as we do a night landscape. Here plants of dramatic shape are positioned to be silhouetted, playing with reflections of light and water. Where winds howl should we not relinquish tortured plants and design a garden of sculptured earth and grasses?

Is this the moment to fuse art and architecture? As gardeners we generally expect art to be subservient to horticulture, but in confined spaces, maybe the roles should be reversed.

In Honolulu, in a square, green-grassed cloister, variously sized floats of psychedelic glass were haphazardly placed by American artist Dale Chihuly, their vibrancy shaming any flower. He had created a space where art dominated vegetation.

A more rugged approach to this concept was taken by another American, landscape designer Topher Delaney, with rocks of blue glass placed on a bed of moss mounds.

In a grassed cloister in Hawaii, American artist Dale Chihuly has installed glass floats to replace the expected flowers.

Glowing and moody in the courtyard of a suburban Californian house, by night they became practical lighting, illuminating the entrance.

Perhaps our 21st-century mission is to release our gardens from a superimposed sameness, to preserve the best of a fragile landscape while allowing diversity to enter, ensuring that our patch of earth is still relevant to its locality as well as to our time and lifestyle. As we travel it is inevitable that we will still impose some of our personal heritage, but ideally we should plan to leave behind a garden that will make for a harmonious relationship between man and the environment around him.

ABOVE *The giant water-lily pads pale into insignificance beside brilliant glass balls created by Dale Chihuly. Capturing every prism of light, these colours reflected in the water bring brilliance to a soft green atmosphere.*

RIGHT *Inspired by the water lilies in an Islamic garden, Chihuly's installation in Chicago, Illinois, brings new life to an indoor garden pool. Its dramatic form and colour eclipse the poolside planting.*

I believe that for a garden design to be harmonious it must be rhythmic. Just as it is delightful to watch the flowing, circling movement in a waltz, so a curve will add softness to a design and a regimented line will seem to compel a smart pace along a path.

I have always liked order and rhythm. Perhaps I have strayed from the Age of Reason, for I delight in the symmetry of the period's architecture and find the perfect metronome precision of a Bach fugue very satisfying. Perhaps this is why I like

garden's most vivid lines to emerge: the vibrant gold, tangerine and burnt-red leaves of the *Nyssa sylvatica* tree which fall straight down like ribbons. They appear as a single line of leaves, so much richer in colour than those behind, and in mature specimens often trail over 6m (20ft).

Vines too can be trained to give strong vertical effects. Within three years a *Clematis montana alba* has covered a 65m (225ft) long pergola at Kennerton Green, tumbling down each column as a line of white

garden rhythm

an avenue of trees to dissect a busy garden, or geometrically placed plants that lead me towards a destination. When planning a garden I like to use plants that by their natural structure or the placement of their flowers or leaves give the suggestions of lines, either parallel or vertical, that seem to provide the idea of movement.

A garden, I believe, needs many rhythms, from the justly famous 'host of golden daffodils' that is a staccato of golden heads, to the soft dense wall of a green hedge, completely harmonious in shape and colour. Each autumn I impatiently wait for one of the

stars and as a patterned curtain from the crossbars above.

A wall of the vigorous vine *Pyrostegia venusta* is like a crashing beat of burnished cymbals catching the sun, for its colour is the most strident brassy orange and its bunches of tubular flowers are overly spectacular

The strong architectural rhythm of the galleries and pergola at Kennerton Green is reinforced by the lines of Clematis montana alba's *star-like flowers. This early-spring picture is accentuated with the flowering of* Rosa 'Wedding Day' *that follows.*

in a warm Sydney garden. But it hangs in absolutely straight lines, like the folds of a curtain. It is a compelling movement that invites exploration into the garden to see what other audacious

colour surprises there might be. I'd love to place a long bench in electric blue or regal purple in front of this cacophony of colour, or tubs of bright blue and purple hydrangeas in season.

Then there are plants with branches that are in spring completely covered with soft leaves and flowers that look like the layered tiers of a white wedding cake. The star of the

The horizontal tiers of Cornus controversa *'Variegata' used dramatically in front of vertical bamboo make a juxtaposition of rhythmic garden forms.*

collection is the most romantic tree, *Cornus controversa* 'Variegata', with softly regimented cream and white leaves and cup-shaped white flower bracts that sit along a branch like well-behaved bridesmaids at the top table. Elegant, with its limbs tapering to a soft conical shape, it is a picture of classic form and symmetry. It is an absurdly dream-like tree, especially when tantalisingly placed on the bend of a path, in the curve of a stream or scattered up a slope; it insists on exploration and creates something more compelling than a major path. Much tougher than it looks, it is happy both in England and in my garden in Australia, where it is withstood a severe drought with only a weekly watering.

Viburnum plicatum 'Lanarth' grows with its lines of flat lacecap flowers in horizontal rows. If planted closely it makes a beautiful hedge to suggest the straight lines of a weatherboard cottage. This planting might seem profligate, for these large shrubs are generally specimen plants, but the effect of such a hedge in Mittagong has been one of the most captivating.

Behind a large birdcage that's covered with a bonnet of tiny double white *Rosa banksiae* is a wall of *Viburnum plicatum* 'Mariesii'. Similar in form to *V. p.* 'Lanarth', but with the bonus of autumn leaf tints, it gallantly withstands weather extremes to make a linear, pretty and decorous foil to the frivolous structure in front. To see the brilliant parrots flash before this wall of white is one of gardening's most extraordinary pictures. In fact, the movement of birds, especially fantail pigeons, peacocks and pheasants, adds activity of its own to a garden.

Another plant with a less defined horizontal effect is the metal-black *Sambucus nigra* 'Black Beauty', or elder, covered with inky dissected leaves that are often likened to those of a Japanese maple. It has flat heads of flowers and dark damson-shaded berries to make a plant of powerful colour. Pruning it right back each year to keep its shape ensures the new flowers and leaves are at eye height.

The ferny foliage and pink horizontal saucer flowers provide background rhythm for other plants. Against this suggestion of parallel lines I've introduced flowers to give a jewel box effect, perhaps an impression of rich gem tones emerging from a murky box. In opposing vertical lines, the tall wide sword leaves of an *Iris germanica* look strong, interplanted with the equally tall drumsticks of alliums. I've mixed ink-blue *Iris* 'Titan Glory' with rich purple *Allium* 'Globe Master'; they flower simultaneously above a mound of *Geranium pratense* 'Victor Reiter Junior', a violet flower from deep foliage.

The creamy lime bracts perched above fresh spring-green leaves make the *Cornus kousa* a tree of exceptional colour, like iced sherbet. A nearly definitive horizontal formation, grown along a drive in spaced groups of three or more its outstretched branches seem to be welcoming and directing towards a destination or a view.

Beneath, I like to plant groups of perennials with definite vertical lines in either leaf or flower against the contrasting forms above, but this time they are fine slim plants in harmonising colour. *Sisyrinchium striatum* 'Variegatum' grows in drifts in dappled light, with rapier-like green and white leaves and poker-stiff flower stems punctuated by light creamy yellow single flowers. Beside it rise the upright stems of *Astrantia*

LEFT *Dramatic architectural circles softened by vines, ferns, hostas and spring perennials make the strongest rhythmic approach across an entry path.*

RIGHT *Using a softer material of woodland saplings, these curved arches create a more informal look. The planting of strong stands of grass echoes this gentler approach to garden architecture.*

major 'Celtic Star', a newer, larger form with a white ruff above lacy green leaves. *Convallaria*, the white, bell-shaped lily of the valley that emerges from soft green leaves, is a must in this cool shade, as is the early-spring *Epimedium* x *versicolor* 'Sulphureum', a lime flower in tune with the tree above.

A planting gets just too busy if there is only wave after wave of flower; a design is much more subtle if there are groups of leaves or of plants that are delicately undemanding. One of my favourites is the slender lines of *Tellima grandiflora* Rubra Group, with its

unimportant green bells just touched with pink above soft flat leaves. In cooler climates I like to introduce a *Tiarella* to this combination, perhaps *T.* 'Neon Lights' with its wondrously marked leaves and its 45cm (18in) rods of upright cloudy cream flowers. But *Tiarella* leaves crisp and burn once warm sun touches them in Mittagong, where they must creep away and hide in the shadiest part of the bed.

All the plants I've placed beneath the *Cornus kousa* trees are mono-chromatic, to create from treetop to the growing shagpile carpet below a planting storey using variations of one colour. It is a soft mood, but garden rhythm can be very hypnotic when striking colour combinations are repeated over and over again.

I'd think long and hard before planting out strong colour in repeated permanent patterns, for though at first glance strong forms and colour excite, excitement is a fleeting emotion.

Golds and burgundies make very strong harmonies. This brilliance could be repeated in a rich line-up of gold leaves: *Robinia pseudoacacia* 'Frisia', a small tough tree, and *Physocarpus opulifolius* 'Dart's Gold' and *Abelia* x *grandiflora* 'Goldstrike', two golden shrubs with contrasting shape and texture in their foliage.

More summer yellow could be introduced in *Hemerocallis* 'Mission Moonlight' and the yellow bracts of *Euphorbia characias*. Both are medium-sized perennials with strong forms.

Burgundy is lit by these colours, and clipped balls of *Berberis thunbergii* f. *atropurpurea* and the small *Acer palmatum* 'Crimson Queen' would look as if they were floodlit. To achieve a continuous rhythm, the plant groupings need to be repeated many times; even more forcible would be a mirror planting on either side of a path.

If these colours were in my garden, I'd break them with tones of fire: the small red-hot poker *Kniphofia* 'Nancy's Red'; an orange dahlia with burgundy leaves, *D.* 'David Howard'; a canna that looks as if it's escaped from a Mexican fiesta, *Canna* var. *phasion* 'Tropicana', the most OTT plant I know. All these would both soften and enliven this rhythm of colour.

Flowing water for me is the ultimate rhythm. I still delight in dropping a blossom or small leaf into a stream and watching it float away in the current. It has always been my dream to have a garden with a natural stream, but to grant my yet-to-be-fulfilled wish I have now made streams with pumping systems. To emphasise the water's rhythm, the stream bed has pebbles placed to resemble the flow. Positioned in curving bands of different sizes, they are coiled into whirlpools and extended curves so that only a small stream of water is needed to create an illusion. These are not works of art but rustic efforts, made from coloured stones and pebbles from a garden centre; it was, I must admit, a time-consuming exercise, but great fun.

My planting design further enhances the idea of movement. Here I use plants with wispy, feathery flowers to catch and flow with the breeze, again extending the suggestion of rhythm. The 45cm (18in) lavender-pink *Astilbe*

LEFT *Clipped hedges that form a sensuous curve make green garden rhythm. The different greens and textures of the plants define the design idea.*

RIGHT & BELOW *Designed by Richard Taylor of Nicholas Tripp Associates for the 2004 Chelsea Flower Show, this rhythmic planting used just clipped box, santolina and the dark leaves of heuchera.*

chinensis 'Veronica Klose' is like streamside fluff in long waterside groups. There are many astilbe varieties available, from ruby pink to white, many growing to 120cm (4ft). All have this graceful vision of lightness and, even though they prefer a well-watered soil, they will tolerate quite dry summers, but not happily.

Taller and more dramatic plants are the rodgersias, which also like moist conditions. They too have panicles of tiny flowers in pyramid form that give an ethereal illusion. 'Structural magnificence' describes the goat's

beard, *Aruncus dioicus*, which again has cream flowers that seem to float.

We have seen wind create ripples through fields of wheat, and grasses nearly prostrate before the wind on the seaside dunes. So grasses too with their fine leaves can catch the light breezes and suggest movement beside a dry creek bed. It is said that the plumed seed heads of *Deschampsia cespitosa* 'Bronzeschleier' are so ethereal they never seem quite in focus, and perhaps 'sweeping silk' could best describe *Stipa tenuissima*, whose form is pure fragility. Unless decimated by snow, many grasses look beautiful all winter, to be trimmed back only when they become rank. To make grasses even more magical, random plant an aquilegia not quite as tall – perhaps

Bold waves of graded coloured pebbles make this path an important garden feature in an already colourful planting. This is an example of just how dominant hard landscape features can be.

dark, double red *A.* 'Double Rubies' – in *Miscanthus sinensis* 'Flamingo'.

But all this flowing rhythm can be boring without firm no-nonsense structure, as in avenues, hedges or solid silhouettes that will make the garden pause before it rushes on again.

Tall and static, the stately, dark, columnar *Cupressus* trees beside fields of grass and flowers give huge drama to the Italian countryside. Singly, as melancholy fingers, they can create a garden's focus; or, when placed at intervals, they move the eye to a vista.

Dark solid shapes can become the defining rhythm of a long flowering border. They do not need to be enormous; in fact clipped geometric shapes no more than 120cm (4ft) high achieve this for me in the long border at Kennerton Green. I made the structures from fine chicken wire, the

tallest 120cm (4ft) high, the balls 90cm (3ft) spheres filled with *Buxus sempervirens*. They remain green forms until the perennials return.

Of course hard architecture creates the strongest rhythm: the straight path, a flight of stairs, the power of a long pergola, the curve of a retaining wall, the parallel lines of tunnels and arches. How definite the beat will be depends on the solidity of the materials chosen. Steps in random bush rock will not be as important as ones of marble; a grass path is gentle, while one decorated by patterns of mosaic tiles will dominate everything. Similarly, a pergola of rustic branches will eventually seem to disappear into the atmosphere, but columns of concrete or stone will be as important as a triumphal procession.

I generally err on the side of not too much hard landscaping, relying more on my plants' natural shapes and the configurations I've made with them to create different aspects of rhythm. At season's end when the leaves are gone and the borders cut away, it is the hard surfaces and permanent evergreens planted to create rhythm that affirm the garden. Through careful placement they will still manipulate the eye to delineate, be it by path, architectural structure, hedge or avenue, the main axis of the garden, keeping the rhythm beating even after the singers have departed.

If I were starting a garden again today, I would assemble the 'brilliant ideas' I wished to include in my design, whether they were gleaned from drawings of historic gardens, snapshots of design features I'd admired on holiday or written notes inspired by plant combinations. Then I'd stop and detail everything I knew about the area where I wished to garden.

* the temperature zone
* average rainfall
* prevailing winds
* soil type and colour

starting from scratch

* the land's topography
* the area's indigenous culture
* the landscape beyond – am I looking into a blank wall, a village street, or far distant hills?
* the immediate view – neighbouring fences, windows, roads
* the space my family needs

Collecting the dog, I'd drive to a nearby street of fine gardens, park, and then the dog and I would spend a pleasant hour looking across them. Local gardens offer many practical clues as to which plants grow successfully, especially for hedging material and fast-growing trees for windbreaks and screening. Talk to the gardeners and ask what other plants succeed locally.

But local fashion can also be misleading. In the Southern Highlands of New South Wales, *Cotinus coggygria* grows brilliantly. In fact it surrounds so many gardens, it would seem to be the best hedging plant to use. I have to confess it's my least favourite plant, as I feel that its new red leaves look uninviting when the temperature rises.

There are also other factors to consider. Although your chosen area will be in a particular climate zone, there are small variations even within a few miles. A range of hills can create shade pockets and microclimates, or a valley can tunnel strong winds.

Make friends with a knowledgeable nurseryman and listen to his suggestions. Local authorities have lists of native vegetation. I obtained advice

This severe design is a complex exercise in hard landscaping that will soon be softened by trees, fountains and moving water (see p. 78).

from the local council for my Hampshire garden, which proved wonderful; in five years a sparse piece of woodland has become robust and quite full of indigenous trees.

It has to be admitted that there are times in our lives when a garden must take second place and too much garden becomes a nightmare. In those early days, fate put me into a house surrounded by large acreage. Here I'd simply make wide terraces around the house and then firmly put the extended garden down to grass and trees that did not need constant water, until I had more time again.

I know that low-maintenance gardening is a fantasy, for paths and terraces must still be swept, 'low-maintenance' ground covers trimmed and encroaching weeds eradicated. Creepers covering walls and trellises must be controlled and grass needs to be mown for six months of the year.

The first garden I ever made was a wide paved terrace outside the kitchen door, surrounded by panels of Victorian wrought iron. It was in southern New South Wales and I knew absolutely nothing about gardening. Into the paving I placed random beds, filled with the toughest Mediterranean plants, for I knew water was at a premium and only this group would survive.

I loved it, for it was a barrier against the burnt landscape beyond. Eventually, as I became more confident, a larger garden emerged, but the back terrace with its small manageable beds always looked bright, for I could easily find a half-hour to weed and plant one square, whereas two days had to be dedicated to cleaning up one of the new extended borders.

Armed with local information, forewarned of perils and inspired to the hilt, I'd review one final question before I put pen to paper: how much will this garden I desire enhance my life? In other words, what do I need for children, outdoor entertainment, pets, deliveries and getting into the kitchen dry? For an older gardener, are there too many levels or steps, and are the surfaces friendly? Are there sheltered spaces to sit and dream? There is no use maintaining a swimming pool or tennis court if it is not used. West Green House's pool became a chequerboard garden.

I'd build my gardens in layers: hard landscape, then major plants, with a definite pause to reconsider, for it's easier to add than to subtract. Once a wall, pool, pergola, path or any other hard-landscaping feature is laid, serious time and money have been expended and it will cause major angst to remove.

This also happens with planting. Of course it's impossible never to slip, as I did not long ago when I planted a hedge of *Camellia sasanqua* in front of a

The strong garden architecture of the ascending steps at Titoke Point, New Zealand, is reinforced by a rhythmic colour planting of coloured acers, precisely placed to urge us along – in the nicest possible way.

rendered wall. I knew camellias loathed lime, but in my haste to hide the wall I planted too quickly. The lime from the render seeped into the ground, and I lost 30 medium-sized bushes.

Allow time to stop and consider carefully when choosing the plant or decorative object for an important position. Once you are assured that it's compatible with the mood of your landscape, it must most importantly issue the famous Mae West invitation, 'Come up and see me sometime.'

There are plants that just ooze such an invitation. In dry warm Mediterranean climates, without humidity, the long slender-leaved hakea grows with flowers that look like sea urchins, some varieties in the most beautiful sugar pink. It makes a wondrously dense screening plant to enclose a courtyard, and is irresistible, especially to children, who cannot refrain from touching the exquisite flowers to see whether they are hard or soft pincushions.

hard landscaping

It is often said that formal gardens are static, moribund, frozen in time. I disagree, for I think they offer the stability of a soft framework within which to paint our ephemeral garden pictures. What is over-monumental is too much hard landscaping. Certainly, we do need sensible paths, drives and some retaining walls, but too many hard surfaces can overpower, especially in winter, when leaves, fronds and flowers are gone.

Stones either as dry walling or cut in blocks are more mellow than bricks, especially cream bricks that never age properly – even five years on, a terrace garden, however beautifully crafted, will still look like a brickies' ad. Where the ground is steep and terracing is imperative, I like to hide my retaining walls by planting a hedge in front, so that when I look up all I see is stepped walls of green, a much more amicable background for flowers, and of course if the plant choice is evergreen the view will still be beautiful in winter.

The first garden space I was given to plant was on top of a gravelly ridge, where, when it rained, topsoil, mulch and new planting just slipped into the dam below. The topography had never been considered. Terraces and retaining walls would have alleviated this dilemma. It was an expensive lesson learnt, which I then applied to a beach-cliff garden on Dangar Island, New South Wales. Here terraces restrained sandy soil and run-off from the sub-tropical storms. (However, the cottage had been built on a barely covered swamp, with a water table that was visible in wet seasons at the bottom of a planting hole. This provided another lesson on drainage: streams, springs and swamps can all be marshalled and exploited to enhance a design, but if not recognised they can also create disasters.)

I like the terrace level that meets the skyline to offer a softer, more transparent texture. This can be achieved with pleached leaves of a deciduous tree, which make a graceful transitional storey and are not as bulky as traditional yew, box or holly used as hedging plants.

In Europe, lime and hornbeam are firm favourites for pleaching, but in my hotter homeland, the lime has been a huge disappointment, as it stresses badly in late-summer heat. The early-spring *Malus floribunda*, with its multitudinous single shell-pink flowers and deep crimson buds, is forming a wall of spectacular pleached blossom for me. This is a very forgiving tree, accepting cold, heat and drought, and coming into flower during spring's earliest days, making its wide band of pink ever more memorable in a bare garden. Most trees and bushes can be trained and shaped, so take note of the lexicon of plants in your area and try for a local look. It will cause more admiring comment than the accepted exotic tree.

For those of us who worry about hard landscaping, green architecture can strike the correct compromise. I find a slope of terraces overpowering, but new earthwork cut to make a terrace does not have to be covered in stone, brick or cement. If the ground is not of a crumbly material, wire netting can be stretched across and a ground-hugging plant – perhaps *Parthenocissus quinquefolia* var. *engelmannii,* a Virginia creeper, self-clinging and autumn scarlet – put in. At West Green House one deep earth ledge is being covered by a yew hedge, another with box, a third with mounds of roses. Walls and arches can be made from most hedging materials.

One hard-landscaping feature that I find essential is a paved terrace adjoining the house. I believe terraces give a house space, providing a platform for windows to open on to, promoting the feeling that there is room for everyone to stretch and breathe. A terrace seems more graceful if it is connected to the rest of the garden by low shallow strips. If space permits, I like to walk from house to

The windows and doors of garden designer Arabella Lennox-Boyd's house in northern England open on to a wide pathed terrace, softened by abundant planting that spills over its hard texture. It makes a compelling area in which to relax while firmly anchoring the house in its own space, before the garden falls away below.

terrace, then to a second terrace and on into the garden.

I like to soften terrace paving with lines of another paving texture, but most of all I like to scatter seeds in the paving cracks. To do this, I lay paving stones on rammed earth with sand falling between the crevices. Here seeds lodge or small plants can be tucked in. There is a wide choice of small plants to dress the floor. Alyssum, a tough sun-loving ground cover tight with tiny flowers, seeds eternally. Lobelia can also self-seed, reappearing in gravel each season. Choose a compact variety like *Lobelia erinus compacta* 'Blue Moon'. Many of the evergreen thymes are tough and release their aroma when trodden on. The tiny lavender flowers of thrift and, with its scent of cloves, dianthus are

tough and drought-forgiving. In cooler climates arabis will make the most delicate white flower mats, with grey foliage and tiny spikes of soft flowers in spring.

Unless there is really not enough space, a terrace should be wide enough for a table and chairs. Of course if it is far above the ground, a balustrade is inevitable. At Whatley Manor in Wiltshire, a terrace is surrounded by a hollow hip-height wall filled with water, aquatic plants and fish, so that the encircling balustrade of the terrace forms a water garden. Moving water, fish and water lilies offer hours of fascination and can be far more entertaining than a traditional dry-wall planting.

water

Water in the garden or courtyard is irresistible, so a pool or fountain will automatically become a focal point. Water as jets, moving in canals, falling from basins, will capture any light, becoming a shining mirror in sunlight. I know that even spying it from afar people will gravitate to it, for water is seductive.

In the USA, the inspirational Martha Schwartz reached back to the ancient irrigation grid of the Middle Eastern garden and created a courtyard composed of wide rills broken by square fountain wells, their depth bathed by coloured light at night and enlivened by slim jets of water. At regular intervals the intervening squares are punctuated by mature *Malus* trees, their roots hidden by more squares of broken white stone, their branches softening the harsh textures of gravel surface, brilliant tiled channels and brick platforms. It is sleek, modern and exhilarating, based on design principles as old as time.

Water in all its moods titillates every emotion and is perhaps one of the most elusive elements to master. Water that does not capture light is dark and depressing, a horrid truth in many an urban courtyard – too much shade just creates murky black sinks. I like water to move, as it seems more cooling and fresh, so even glassy water should be kept alive with a small pump. With problematic water that I've given up on, I simply introduce a blanket of water lilies to cover it, often breaking their leaves' flat surface with important groups of water iris. This is a good idea anyway, as it will extend the flowering season in the pond to over five months.

In Michael Likkerman's garden, near Menton in southern France, two small concentric pools of water surrounded a central ornament. The still water closest to the pedestal was literally choked with pale pink lotus, rising to 120cm (4ft) above pale green leaves; the outer circle was dense with flat water-lily pads, softening the focal sculpture and turning doubtful captured water into a pool of beauty.

Water lilies are the most satisfactory plant, for different varieties will grow wild – from the tiny pale stars found in central Sweden to the magnetic blue hues of the swamps of Kakadu National Park in northern Australia. Their pads can be large, forming shiny skating rinks for small frogs, or miniature in leaf and flower to enhance the smallest bowl.

Many years ago, I saw a French movie called *Mon Oncle*. It was hilarious, and most memorable was a fountain that was supposed to work when visitors arrived. Of course it didn't, and made unfortunate sounds instead. I always think of this when I see exhibition gardens that have hot steam covering rocks or curling through bamboo, or modern water fountains with synchronised jets – all stunning concepts, but will they always work? So whatever effects we choose they must be practical and fixable.

Water falling as a shining skin down geometric objects, sculptures and steps gives the impression of glittering light, and is deeply delightful, but freely moving water creates its own sound, a bonus to disguise urban noise – or an embarrassment in a too-enclosed place where conversation is desired. Small water features seem to be more appealing if they have a degree of formality. A small rill or wider canal or pond placed in direct sunlight will capture the sky's moods.

Naturalistic water features I believe look best in large landscapes planted as simply as possible. I am of the school that is in awe of sylvan waters set in a grassed landscape that pays homage to Alexander Pope's dictum: serenely romantic with one perfectly proportioned object to attract the eye.

I find the giant leaves of a massive group of water's-edge *Gunnera manicata* forming secret places in summer irresistible, and a stand of trees in bonfire colour gives essential reflected drama by water in autumn. Smaller ponds, planted with mixed jumbles of marginal planting, often seem like grandmother's crocheted doily – too frilly and unnecessarily concealing the sheen beneath, and worse – but a connecting series of ponds fringed with impossibly lacy massed candelabra primulas one chill spring morning in England afforded a sublime gardening moment of intense beauty.

For centuries, great gardens have been adorned with tall arches and columns for static decorative height, but a forest of poles in glass became fountains at the Festival International des Jardins at Château Chaumont in the Loire in 1999, brilliant coloured height that was a modern *tour de force* of hard landscaping. And the most exciting use of trees to add height to a major new garden design has been for me the trees that rise from a sea of moving water created by American designer Dan Kiley for the Fountain Plaza in Dallas.

The garden I covet more than any other is Mas de les Voltes, in Gerona in northern Spain, the work of the Spanish designer Fernando Caruncho. Here an entire landscape composed of wheat, olives, vines and water is dominated by fingers of stark, still, columnar Cupressus that cross all the design elements in co-ordinating lines, their precise beauty ultimately reflected in the giant pools of water.

When I first started gardening, planning a new garden or bed was easy, for I knew absolutely nothing about theory, whether plants were suitable to grow together or not, and borrowed vistas, sightlines and levels were unheard of.

Somehow, eventually, it all worked, but now, older and wiser and with decided preferences, I agonised over my two new permanent gardens, delaying for years as I vacillated between too many ideas. What has resulted encapsulates my enthusiasms –

intertwined branches were heavy with ripe fruits, so that whenever the windy host passed through them, the fruits dropped on the water, while birds of all kinds swooped down after them, clapping their wings and singing. To the right and left of the pond stood couches of sandalwood covered with silver.'

In early Islamic and Christian cultures the enclosed garden was paradise. In Greek the word is *paradeisos*, derived from the Persian *pairidaeza*, literally meaning

the old city square in Cordoba, where orange trees surrounded by round basins form a geometric grid joined by shallow brick rills of flowing water.

In Marrakesh's historic Medina the grand geometric pattern becomes a Ryad's simple garden of paradise: just a square courtyard of four beds with a central fountain, captured by three-storey walls, where under dappled light through the canopy of scented orange trees the family relax, meet and entertain. It echoes with life and laughter, and the memories of rose

a new garden – scheherazade's paradise

for water, geometry and minimalist simplicity.

It is so long ago now – one could be justified in saying 'once upon a time' – that the ballet *Scheherazade,* danced to the sensuous music of Rimsky-Korsakov, transported a country child into a vision of silvered minarets and gossamer veils as the story unfolded in a most wondrous garden. Years later I read *The Arabian Nights* and the description of the garden: 'The water flowed from a large pond to a smaller one, surrounded with sweet basil, lilies and narcissus in pots of inlaid gold… thickly

'surrounded by walls'. For the Muslim these gardens wove together spiritual and secular pleasures, creating paradise on earth.

In Mediterranean lands, famous examples and urban re-creations of these sensory gardens exist. Within Granada's fourteenth-century Alhambra Palace, the Long Canal, now rippling under the gauze spray from a line of single water spouts (a nineteenth-century addition), has been secure for hundreds of years in its long rectangular space, framed by tile-capped walls and graceful filigreed arches. An even more evocative space is

petals scattered each evening in the tiny central fountain, and of the flickering candlelight on shiny tiles, sent me home to make my own vision of paradise. To an Australian living in the driest continent, the idea of a garden walled and protected from the

At the heart of the Majorelle garden, Marrakesh, Morocco, a rectangular pool with a central fountain playing water to cool the air is surrounded by plants suited to the harsh environment. Open to the public, the Majorelle explicitly illustrates the Islamic concept of a paradise garden.

harshest elements, sheltered by the shade of trees and watered by fountains and streams of running water, sounded like Elysium.

A collection of ugly government buildings next to my garden at Kennerton Green came on the market. Surrounded by black asphalt, these products of 1950s design had nothing to recommend them – except that with modification they could become the sides of a courtyard. Now, three years later, they have been entirely rebuilt with new doors and windows opening onto a courtyard cooled by precise streams of water around herb gardens. The verandas are hung with jasmine which in the evening saturates the garden with the fragrance that is a vital element of those gardens conceived as a foretaste of heaven.

In Penelope Hobhouse's *Plants in Garden History*, I found two illustrations, one from a fifteenth-century Mogul poem 'Halnamah', the other a miniature dated 1010–15 showing two friends meeting at the intersection of two canals. These painted gardens of idealised perfection were my design inspiration, so it was very fitting that Penelope gave the first lecture here, for these once-ugly buildings are now a gallery and library where we meet and talk gardening.

My starting point was the grid design for the water rills. As in the miniature, the water flowed from large square basins to smaller ones, intersecting to form a nearly square pattern of eight sections. One of the Mogul miniatures shows the small canals as terracotta-coloured, so I purchased half-terracotta water pipes and outlined the pond edges in local sandstone.

The illustrations show the waterways and basins outlined again. My guess is that this outline may have been in sand or gravel, for this is the colour in the picture, but I did these paths in levels of clipped grass. It looked very smart newly done, but it is an intensive job to maintain, so is going to have to be replaced!

A design based on irrigated water has to be absolutely flat to ensure the water's continuous flow. In past times the beds would have been slightly below the water level of the rills, for water was used for serious irrigation as well as ornament. Height was provided in Middle Eastern gardens by architecturally exhilarating pavilions, platforms and, of course, trees. Translating this concept into the centre of utilitarian buildings in New South Wales called for a more cautious approach to decoration. My choice for height was four large 95cm (40in) square pots, one in each of the four central squares. Here again I was bowing my head to tradition,

In a fantasy herb potager, aromatic mint, agastache and rose petals in dishes inscribed with Moroccon verse are captured inside a dense hedge so that their fragrance will be held within the garden.

observing the geometry of an Islamic garden, constructed in multiples of four, a number Muslims infused with symbolism.

Citrus trees – lemons or oranges – were destined for the pots. The trees arrived, then left, for visually the round geometry of the trees didn't work: the severe edges of the buildings, rills and paving needed softness, so I tried weeping birch trees, *Betula pendula*. They created the gentle effect of willows above a stream, sighing in the breeze, their light green leaves always gentle coolness. Definitely not traditional, but the effect is heavenly.

An electric pump, with the return water tank hidden beneath a herb bed, pumps the water along the rills. Small submerged pumps create bubbling jets in the two large square basins, and at

night the entire design is lit by underwater lights, for summer fire bans negate any ideas of flickering candles or flaming torches!

In John Harvey's *Medieval Gardens*, a list of plants compiled by the eleventh-century Muslim botanist al Birni names primarily Mediterranean-zone plants. Many of these are suitable for the Mittagong climate, and the plants I selected were from this list – fruit trees and fragrant herbs. But for a gardener besotted by colour, the selected plants also had to complement the hues of the surrounding walls, fences and the countryside beyond.

Eucalyptus-green paint covers the walls; two shades of lavender and purple brighten the railings and seats, with silver grey on columns and edges. Four garden beds, two at either end of the regular pattern, were planted with low-growing herbs chosen for their white, lavender and blue flowers, all easily replaceable, for most herbs are either annual or biennial. Perfume was very important to my plan, with herbs, especially mint, giving noonday fragrance in protected spaces.

Although the planting will change each season, I always include:

- Catmint (*Nepeta mussinii*) has the softest frilled grey leaves and the most heavenly blue flowers and musky scent all summer. It needs a hard prune at the season's end.
- **Rosemary** (*Rosmarinus officinalis*) is one of the most aromatic plants, with tough fine leaves and tiny blue flowers in spring. Simply clip it to keep it at the height and shape required.
- **Sage** (*Salvia officinalis*) is well known for the downy flat grey-green leaves used in traditional stuffing, but by mid summer it has bright blue flowers and is deeply fragrant. I find sage plants prefer to be pinched back: cutting into the older wood often kills the plant.
- **Thyme** (*Thymus vulgaris* 'Silver Posie') is neat and tidy with silver-backed small leaves, and in summer it is simply smotheredwith lavender-pink flowers. If it gets too rampant I simply trim it back.
- **Violas and pansies** (*Viola* spp.): I know they are a spring cliché but they pack a colour punch beneath the grey-green foliage of herbs. Nurseries offer selections of mixed blues under multiple names, which will grow in most climates, performing from spring for four months.

I have described the simplest garden: regular square beds and everyday herbs and colours – a blueprint taken from the ancient irrigated garden. It captured nothing of the voluptuous Scheherazade's 'paradise' nor of the feeling of those intense patterns and colours that created the opulence of a Matisse odalisque reclining in a suggested Islamic garden. My garden cried out for an overlay of colour, texture and form to give it soul, emotion and, I hoped, a seductive element.

Large hexagonal tubs of *Lavandula* x *allardii*, a tall Australian lavender that thrives in the courtyard sun, and the contoured boughs of *Cupressus*, in trees already 3.5m (12ft) tall, are evocative of Mediterranean gardens that have broken the flat surface of the surrounding path. Persian sumptuousness came in the nineteenth-century tiles, a keepsake of a long-forgotten British army officer, depicting in glazed blues, lavender, yellow and green, two reclining figures in a field of flowers – said to have been inspired by *The Rubáiyát of Omar Khayyám*. Australian artist Greg Daly fired shades of greens and gold leaf into four 75cm (2½ft) extravagant wall plates. In pots on verdigris tables, *Tulipa* 'Blue Parrot' and later china-blue Dutch iris add early flowers.

Roses were an essential ingredient of the Mogul garden, and for days I agonised over whether to introduce fragrance through a 'blue herb' bed or one of roses. Because of the warmth that would be held within the

LEFT *My initial
design for the
paradise garden at
Kennerton Green.*

KEY

blue herbs

lavender

cypress

silver birch

small basins

fountains

canals

grass

paths

courtyard I opted to plant herbs, but a terrace above will hold a 'Persian carpet' design that includes roses.

Many 'Persian carpet' designs are stylised interpretations of paradise gardens. To look down on a Persian carpet is to see a mixture of reds, pinks, magentas and inky blues in a flat intricate pattern of formal shapes. The garden can be oblong, like most carpets. The carpet borders can be planted in a mass of ground-cover roses. The ground-hugging *Rosa* 'Raubritter' has superb rich pink cups of flowers; flowering once only, it is one of the finest roses, as is deep magenta *R.* 'Magic Carpet', which forms another wide band. As summer passes, annuals come through to replace the roses, mimicking the random flowers in a traditional rug

LEFT *The edges of a central fountain in the new paradise garden at Kennerton Green are softened by flowering thyme and sage, their colour heightened by small clumps of blue pansies. Here too the perfume is captured, this time by high walls, to ensure a fragrant garden.*

RIGHT *To reinforce the precise pattern of the graph-paper grid of rills, huge square planters holding weeping birch, oblong troughs of lavender, even diagonally slatted chairs were chosen.*

OVERLEAF *Elements that create the aura of scrumptiousness in my paradise garden in Australia: left, the old Persian tiles with decoration inspired by* The Rubáiyát of Omar Khayyám; *centre, pools of water with fountain plates designed by Greg Daly; right, a medley of purples, golds, blues and eucalyptus green seems at home under the Australian skies and is echoed in the plants and hard landscaping of the garden.*

design — stiff zinnias, their flat faces liking the same hot sun as roses. English gardeners may be doubtful whether zinnias will succeed, but Sarah Raven is adamant that her zinnia seeds enjoy the English summer.

Lavandula stoechas, a compact 30–60cm (1–2ft) lavender of regal purple with a long-petalled topknot, and *Lysimachia atropurpurea*, with fat 45cm (18in) spikes of Beaujolais colour, are combined with a dark-leaved heuchera to add even deeper tones to the carpet. The last two are perennials that will form good clumps quickly. Buy erect marigold seedlings, perhaps a selection of vanilla, gold and orange, and a yellow variety called *Calendula* 'Doubloon' to provide other colours or forms to be found in these famous carpets, and splash them through *Heliotropium* 'Cherry Pie', deeply purple and powerfully scented, again growing to 30–60cm (1–2ft).

I like to keep the flowers in my carpet as even in height as possible, but *Verbena bonariensis* would add purple architecture in mid summer, as would *Salvia nemorosa* 'Amethyst', a 90cm (3ft) fusion of red and pink spikes, and achillea's flat saucers of tiny upward-facing flowers. Achillea has fallen victim to a succession of wet English autumns and winters and is now often treated as an annual; it is a perennial in warm climates. I like *A. millefolium* 'Sammetriese', the faded red of an old Turkish carpet and a perfect designer colour.

Fruit is trained to the walls. My carpet would be secure within walls where lemons, espaliered as fans, join Brown Turkey figs in cordons, as do plums, their feet kept warm by round clipped balls of santolina and rosemary, making a colour pattern in two shades of grey; all choices for a warm-climate garden.

Great doors and powerful gates kept these gardens hidden away from curious ancient eyes. My garden is entered through a plain barred gate from a colonnade of grey masonry pillars absolutely smothered in snow-white *Clematis montana*, its flowering followed by *Rosa* 'Wedding Day', a favourite white rambler. They are a perfect continuing story, for they both have simple single flowers, ensuring that the entrance is blanketed in a cloud of floral snow for four months.

From the gate, two lines of cream sandstone pots form an honour guard of clipped orange-fruiting kumquats, their toes covered in intense deep blue *Lobelia* 'Crystal Palace'. Diamonds of silver-grey *Lavandula* 'Munstead' clipped as low hedges enclose the pots and hold back summer-flowering *Salvia stratum*, its furry silver-white spikes studded by blue flowers.

White-blossoming espaliered plum trees trained in simple cordons back this display of orange, blue, silver and white, which is tempered by wayward alyssum, self-seeding where it pleases in paths and garden, to appease the rigid geometry.

more visions of water

Patterns of water dance in my head. Trees surrounded by rings of water, this time crab apples arching above carpets of snowdrops, *Galanthus* 'Flore Pleno', would be a concept of paradise for a cool climate – an English version that is finding its way from the drawing board to Hampshire.

The wasteland at West Green House, beyond the tall brick walls where a garden of English floral extravagance infills a parterre pattern, had tantalised and frustrated me for years. Directly to the south of it, deep green yew hedges are cut sharply behind the exposed white trunk of Betula utilis var. jacquemontii, enclosing the most formal Italian water garden, its rill and water steps descending in uniform procession. Then to the west and north, a pastoral scene slopes quickly towards a field of lakes, daffodils and meadows, creating wild beauty as it encircles follies, temples and aviaries in exaggerated classical mode. All the elements of a quintessential English arcadia should, I felt, be represented in this one spot.

Mentally I gathered together the essence of the established gardens – geometric formality, grass, trees and water – to conceive a design that must

The new water garden at West Green House, showing half of the repeating pattern.

KEY

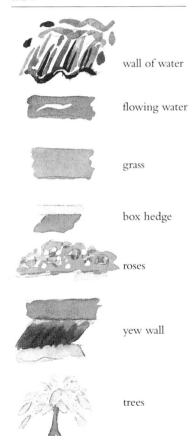

wall of water

flowing water

grass

box hedge

roses

yew wall

trees

act as a transition between them all. I
saw it as a terrace enclosed on three
sides by wall, hedge and wooded
planting, from which to look down
upon the meadows and waterways; a
tranquil place in which to reflect on
the intense garden activity behind,
before refocusing the mind on a
gentler scene.

I started to draw linear beds, but as
I so often find, the pattern began to
take on a life of its own. Small hedges
soon became rills, and set-piece flower
beds turned into fine curtains of mist.
The supposed fountain wells were
now to be planted with trees.

The pattern became more elaborate
as the water lines bent to enclose the

trees, creating six islands. Then it
doubled to become two water
patterns, reflecting each other across
a central swathe of fine lawn.

The design began to please me,
for it was simple in its textures – just
water, trees and grass – and the
complexity of its lines and the
movement of the water would add

LEFT & RIGHT *Stage 2 of West Green House's new water garden (see p. 59) – still to be finished, I am beginning to feel that the design is working!*

the elements of surprise, fun and beauty that are inherent in the West Green House gardens.

But was it achievable? There was only one person in England to ask: Mike Chewter, who has been described as the Rolls-Royce contractor for water gardens.

This is the second project on which Mike and I have collaborated, and as he had done before he hooted with laughter as I presented my design, which was, as usual, on the back of an envelope – all my designs start and finish this way, until I become so embarrassed that I give them to a draftsman to cloak me in respectability.

As with all gardens of geometric proportions and moving water, it was essential that the site was graded billboard-flat before pegs and string measured out the design. Next the rills were excavated, lined first with concrete bricks, then with fibreglass, with a mass of electric cables and water pipes becoming a major event beneath. Finally crisp stone edges, fine grass and island trees created the minimalist design of silver threads of moving water.

Below two sides of the terrace there was just rammed earth, so to deter weeds a shade cloth was stretched across it. A facing of tall trees has been planted at the base of the terrace: this will eventually cover the wall as a solid frame, growing to grass level above.

As I sat and contemplated the new garden I knew that, although it was serene and beautiful, the greens were too tonal. As I had found with the Australian garden, the basic idea was sound but it needed that 'X factor'. And again I was sure it could be supplied by the foliage of the trees.

I searched for *Cornus controversa* 'Variegata' (see p. 50) without success, so 3.5m (12ft) *Malus* 'Red Sentinel' crab apples, with white flowers and deep red fruits, were substituted. Marvellous trees, but in mid summer the greens of the leaves were the same intensity as the surrounding woods, making the whole design pleasing but staid. Now, the search for the trees I originally wanted intensifies, and I have learned that it is better to wait for the best and not settle for less.

Another plant has to be chosen to effect a joining of a precision design to the disparate styles beyond. I know it will be a rose – a wild old variety, perhaps 'Alba Semi-Plena', a moss rose of superb fragrance that looks at home both in captivity and in the wild.

Now I dream of a long couch surrounded at four corners by tall poles in many hues and raised on a platform at the garden's east end. From here one will view the rills on one side and the walled garden on the other. But for once I am pausing, for the mood of the garden will develop and soon I will know if this dream is correct.

Beautiful gardens have always been adorned by statues, urns, fine gates, aviaries, temples, columns, arches, pergolas… It's an endless list of aesthetically satisfying objects. And local garden centres offer us an ever-multiplying array of objects from which to choose.

I must admit I am slightly 'off' objects. Firstly because the same ones seem to reappear everywhere, simply because they are appealing, and secondly because every urn or object I have purchased for West Green House

decoration

has been stolen. In this I am not alone, for many gardens are visited by the light-fingered. So now when I come to select garden decoration I want something unique and if possible permanent, or simply just fun that is not resaleable.

I often feel that lateral thinking produces some of the most amusing and charming garden decorations. In a central Italian garden a small stone bust had the back of its head broken off, so the garden's owner had laid it face up in a tiny pool. Walking across the terrace, looking down on this face encircled by a ruff of water plants, was

The most beautiful antique shepherdess is adorned by a rose plucked from nearby. She stands as the focal point in a rose garden, perfectly in keeping with the style of her surroundings.

surprising and diverting. In a grander English garden, a Victorian bust of a whiskered gentleman emerges shoulder high from a round basin of water.

I much admired this concept, so I translated it into a cut-out timber figure, painted most dramatically by my friend Marcus Williams. It is of Neptune arising from the water, fork in hand. In fact, cut-out figures dress the garden now, rather than statues. This was an adornment favoured in the eighteenth century, so appropriate still in formal design.

At Kennerton Green I was concerned about the safety of a birdcage, so instead of alarming it and investing in other safety devices, I placed it in the middle of a pond. It looks splendid, framed by Louisiana iris in late spring and water lilies in summer; and it is, I think, the most satisfying picture in my garden.

Generally we plan garden paths to be practical, with easy-to-walk-on surfaces, but they can be rather boring. Stone tablets of poetry from favourite sources can enliven a walk or, placed in front of a bench or seat, add more interest to a pause, provoking gentle contemplation too. Clay tablets seem to belong against roots of trees as well as on garden walls. I like to choose my own poetry, as it's more personal than buying popular sayings from garden-centre displays.

The story of St Francis, purchased at a tourist shop in Assisi and intended to be displayed as a panel of wall tiles, found itself inserted into a brick path. A simple idea, and visiting children delight in running ahead to find St Francis with more animals. However, stop to think before inserting too many travel souvenirs into a garden, for are they at odds with your garden's mood?

Often very ordinary garden-centre objects can be recycled into innovative garden delights. In a rash moment I purchased a bench, one of those with sides and a pitched roof. When it arrived it looked less effective than one I already had – so what to do? The solution was to put shelves across it and turn it into an auricula theatre, another gardening idea recycled from previous centuries. Of course, the 'theatre' had to be set on a concrete foundation so that it was safe, and new

ABOVE *A handsome terracotta pot makes a punctuation mark at the end of a long border. It's important to choose objects whose size is in proportion to the position they will occupy.*

OPPOSITE *Garden ornaments can just be good fun. Here, a potager fountain is fashioned from a row of galvanised watering cans.*

pots of primulas are prepared each year. Prized pelargoniums also come forth for the summer.

Commonplace objects can be arranged in diverse and unusual ways. I have used a line of pottery jars to make water spouts that pour into a concrete trough, by running pipes to the holes at their bases. Large brass taps placed in a line on a wall above a trough make utilitarian but attractive fountains, and the fun use of watering cans secured in a line at a pouring angle can make a joyous fountain too.

Recycling can provide a multitude of ideas: old spades, forks and rakes welded together to make a garden gate or as trophies on a wall; sturdy wooden trays mounted on legs to form rustic waist-height herb planters; and those who have a stone trough or sink for alpine plants possess a garden treasure.

Today the workings of clocks are not prohibitively expensive, and I like the idea of a slender clock tower at the end of an allée, or of using the workings in a homely and practical way as a feature on a wall in a vegetable garden. The same function could be served by shiny brass bells.

Fine objects tend to be a major investment and it is a great pleasure to visit gardens where they belong. But with wit and imagination, decoration can be individual and illustrate a garden's message. It will be more dramatic if only a few objects are used – too many ideas dilute any impact. I like to seclude my objects by hiding them in groups of trees or the curve of a hedge, to poke out of odd spaces. They are just added attractions in a garden, but in a courtyard they can be the main event, the 'make or break' feature of the design.

entrances

Entrances set the scene; they are the first indicators of the style of the garden. More than any other decorative feature, they should have some relation to the property. Grandiose gates in front of villas, decorated with cement lions, each with its paw on a ball, enliven many a suburban street in Australia; they proclaim the proud owner's achievement, but overshadow all that is beyond. The white picket fences and gate, evoking the idea of old cottages, in front of new urban brick houses seem out of place too, as does settler post-and-rail fencing, an image of the pastoral homestead.

Inevitably, new fences and gates have to be erected in front of older dwellings. Here I like to cover the new materials with a fast-growing creeper and distress the paint on the gates. But if I need to place a new entrance in front of a modern building, this could be the moment to play with modern design, perhaps using great blocks of coloured Perspex or sheets of brushed metals. But sometimes those heavy doors in walls that offer no clues to the garden beyond, found in many a Mediterranean town are the best advice. For what is more exciting than stepping through a plain gate in a wall or hedge and being transfixed by the beauty within?

2

designing with plants

I grew up in a warm climate surrounded by open grazing land where trees for shade and windbreaks were of great importance. Their placement was also problematical, for while deep-shade trees helped cool the homestead's iron roof, many varieties of hardy eucalyptus were very combustible and placed too close to the house they could be conductors of sparks in times of fires. Then, on a more mundane level, the roots would find nearby drains and clog them, and leaves inevitably filled the gutters.

totally flat, the brown grass dull and lifeless. It was a hot place to escape from on such a burning day. This inhospitable site was where I'd chosen to plant a copse of trees to form a small, naturalised environment that would re-create the endless charm of a wild place.

In a warm climate a grove of trees can create a microclimate, bringing cooling shade to a parched area, providing a canopy for heat-stressed plants. In the northern hemisphere's cooler lands, trees are often expelled to

naturalising trees

So now, when I come to mull over a garden design, one of my very first thoughts is about the type, style and placement of trees.

A woodland glade is not just another name for a group of trees that will often create a garden area with shade problems. It is in fact a different platform for another style of garden design. Here I try to imitate a well-tended wood where the trees have been coppiced to allow light to penetrate, so that the trees form fully but allow flowers and grasses to grow beneath.

My mind goes back to a January day in Australia: the paddock was

a garden's edge as flowering specimens and curios while warmth and the direct sun are welcomed. It was not until I came to live in a cooler climate that I realised the importance of a

Planted in 1991, the birches at Kennerton Green now form a maturing grove of just one species, Betula *'Moss's Variety', above a rotation of just one flower. Here, bluebells colonise where weeks before daffodils flowered, and soon blue irises will replace the thousands of small bulbs.*

tree's bark: many varieties are grown to provide thrilling colour even into the bleakest weather. Never will I forget the lacquer scarlet, on a raw English January day, of multiple stems of *Cornus alba* 'Sibirica' planted tightly together. It was pure garden Technicolor.

As trees must be planted with the knowledge of how they will look in twenty years, their design will not be appreciated until they start to produce some canopy, which can be up to seven to ten years later. Until then the pleasure of this planting will be in the domain beneath.

When one is looking up towards a canopy of trees they all seem to be of the same undulating height, but at ground level it will not be so. Even the flattest forested floor is a series of gullies, some caused by rain and falling trees, or creatures who dig humps and holes, forming ridges that

An entirely new garden to resemble an idealised landscape was created out of farmland at West Green. Here a newly dug lake is crossed by a Chinese-style bridge and a fanciful bird cage is crowned by a pineapple.

enliven the terrain. Here tufted grasses, jagged root stumps, rocks and stones delineate the uneven surface, broken after rain into streams, ponds and boggy ooze, then cracked by temperature extremes in another season.

Young trees start their journey to the light, leaving smaller plants and bushes behind, while rotting logs provide a home for creepers, ferns and fungi and the seasonal carpet of flowers that are the lures to explore these hidden places. When planning a mini wood I have found the first decision the most difficult and also the most fun: what type of tree to plant.

I like to plant the bulk of my trees using just one variety, adding other species to delineate a feature – perhaps to encircle an urn, seat or sculpture, or to outline an allée – then perhaps just one electrifying specimen tree as a stand-alone, a delight in a clearing.

The mind's picture of woodlands is generally that of Sherwood Forest with the latest screen hunk swinging from forest giants, but small plantings of dogwoods, maples, birches, olives, Manchurian pear, all woodland trees in their native habitat, can provide a more manageable domestic canopy for a naturalised floor planted beneath.

The choice of tree will generally determine the landscape design. It can be a selection of native trees, with the forest floor a planting of indigenous species, or an exotic collection, with perhaps a profusion of small bulbs and flowers to cover the roots and decorate the new landscape.

People often scoff at incongruous plantings, such as the most wondrous swathe of daffodils naturalised beneath ancient gum trees in Victoria, Australia. But we do live in what is now called a global village, where everything travels, even our ideas and plants. In what will be perhaps one of the garden's most notable designs – a grouping of trees – should we preserve the difference in our own landscape? An important point to ponder before the design is chosen, but it is also worth remembering that most daffodil species we plant are not indigenous, so Wordsworth's daffodils could be said to be foreign even to Cumbria. Perhaps the perspective of time makes us more accepting. I always stop and remember that many of the trees, bulbs and wild flowers we associate with the northern European woodlands had their origins in countries bordering the Mediterranean. So we, as generations of gardeners have done before us, will plant to indulge our desires but remembering the consequences of maintenance that a differing habitat will bring in establishing exotic trees.

practicalities of trees

As with all planting, ensure the chosen tree will like the climate. Extreme heat causes stress and scorched leaves in a dry climate, so it is vital that there is enough water available to carry so many trees through dry and windy years. Frost, cold and soggy soils add their own problems.

After the bobcat finished creating the space for my new stand of trees, it looked like a Lilliputian landscape: hills of varying size with scooped-out pools, terraces, paths and streams had been carefully planned in scale drawings before these were given to the driver. But here experience speaks: never be too far away from man or machine until the sweep of the last blade, for those who have watched these men at work will know about the amazing interpretations of a plan that can occur.

Water must be available at the site before planting, for young trees need regular watering, as their roots must not be allowed to dry out. Climate dictates just how extensive an irrigation system is required, as does the chequebook. Electricity too is needed for water pumps and any artificial lights, and this is the time to set these services in place. The thought of a rustic ruin amongst the trees or any delectable construction

ideas – streams, ponds, rock formations or classical mounds – should all be sited now, for trees should not be disturbed once planted. Men with trucks do not see new plantings when reversing or unloading, so trees must wait until all hard landscaping is done.

The easiest way to plant a large number of trees is to hire a posthole digger. I like to put two or three saplings in one hole in tight groups among more spaced specimens, trying to create a seemingly haphazard planting that reflects the wild.

A tonal dream world where lines of green plants make the woodland floor a most engaging landscape. The soft shade cast by the tree canopy above allows ferns, hostas and clipped shrubs to make garden pictures below.

In a woodland, the trees are always at different stages of growth, so when purchasing trees, allow for half of the trees to be mature, perhaps up to five years old, then a selection of three-year-old saplings, with the rest as tube stock, to achieve a more natural growth. I have to admit I always plant my groups with species I know will mature within a few years – *Acer, Malus, Cornus* and *Prunus*. Time is not on my side these days.

Plant trees with a good fertiliser mixed at the bottom of a water-filled hole, and then slightly scoop away the earth from the trunk to form a shallow basin. This hollow in a dry climate will encourage water collection. Conversely, I had to raise the planting of nearly 50 yew trees in the damper Hampshire climate, as I had failed to take into consideration the run-off from the fields next door and the new trees were drowning in subsoil water.

This line of new yew trees altered the topography, forming barriers that collected long lakes of moisture. The problem was solved by building a bank 45cm (18in) high and replanting, with agricultural drains installed to drain the water.

Have the soil tested: it's not only that the plants could die – if they don't like their situation they will sulk doing absolutely nothing, whilst years are wasted as you try to decide if they should be moved or replaced.

Watch where any natural springs or storm waters flow and remember this as the new contours are planned. More neighbourhood acrimony arises from diverted water than from parties or dogs! Better still, trap any run-off to create a boggy glade or pool. Poor drainage will kill trees.

When planting the miniature forest floor, the size of the tree's leaf is important. The leaves of *Platanus acerifolia*, the London plane tree, are large and coarse and in autumn will swamp floor plantings in a duvet thickness. Left naturally they will smother any swathe of late-season colchicums or cyclamen. Other trees put out leaves quite late in spring and then in reverse refuse to let go. My liquidambars give an unsurpassed autumn performance, then forget to bow out, so the leaves fall so late that they smother early fritillaries beneath.

The design options for the floor of this sheltered ground are myriad. I like to cover naturalised areas with masses of bulbs, which makes it essential to choose a slow-growing spring grass mix, so that its enthusiasm does not overpower the bulbs. If the floor is to be wild and rough, put selected grasses in large groups in open spaces to reflect forest clearings. Try *Setaria* 'Lowlander' with its brown foxtails together with copper-brown *Carex flagellifera*; these grasses, used with rocks, are just meant for each other's ruggedness.

In Harden, New South Wales, a grove of trees has been planted around a deep hole the size of a large circular bed. A spiral grass path has been cut into its side to wind down to the

bottom. Around its rim randomly placed alders were sited to grow from the edge of the basin walls in a visionary design that could be a compact idea for an urban space.

At Buskers End, a well-tended garden in Bowral, New South Wales, a wild space was left beneath a copse of old pink Japanese flowering cherry trees, their trunks and branches trimmed to show their beauty. They formed sparse cover above a mosaic texture of grasses spiked with sparaxis, those brilliant harlequin bulbs that are as slender as the grass. Planted together they camouflaged the massive shapes of giant pots that had been haphazardly placed beneath the trees. It was an engaging juxtaposition of solid and filmy texture, negating the sometimes too pretty effect that massed cherry trees can give. This unexpected wildness was an island in a suburban garden's manicured lawns, presenting common plants in an unusual way.

A slope or a man-made mound enhances groupings of fragile blossom trees. *Prunus* 'Ukon', the 'green' flowering cherry, looks its best grown in groups as it is a smaller open tree that needs companionship. In tight groups of five or seven trees, so their branches interweave, place them perhaps beside a serpentine path of sandstone, steps snaking through, so the élan of the colour can be closely

observed. I'd forgo an underplanting of soft flowers and sharpen the undergrowth with the lime grass *Milium effusum* 'Aureum', and the dwarf variegated gold bamboo *Pleioblastus variegatus* 'Tsuboii' to reinforce a suggestion of oriental charm. Or, if a softer look is desired, indispensable to this woodland colour would be the palest lemon foxglove *Digitalis lutea*, and in a sunlit clearing *Verbascum chaixii* 'Gainsborough', repeating the upright form but here with button flowers up the stem. From afar these trees would look as a curve of curious colours, so much more consequential than a single tree of spring blossom.

At the Chelsea Flower Show in 2002 I loved the seat that encircled a round Celtic fire pit punctuated by stone backrests, so reminiscent of Stonehenge slabs. As I admired the wild effect of stone and turf, I imagined what a convivial meeting place it could be, enclosed by the wild, rich autumn colour and scarlet berries of a grove of *Crataegus persimilis* 'Prunifolia', a collision of colour and climate on an Indian-summer afternoon. It would be a deep circle within a tree circle, making a hideaway to provide garden secrecy.

We plant trees to give the garden form, structure and height, to obscure the outside world and bring in the

Acer pennsylvanicum – *one of the many maples worth planting for the splendour of its winter bark.*

birds and butterflies. Trees that produce spring flowers and autumn berries are wildlife favourites. Consider a very, very sparse random planting of *Sorbus aucuparia*, the orange-berried rowan – just two or three for dappled light – amongst scarlet poppies, *Papaver shoales*, and the Californian poppy *Eschscholzia californica,* in creams and orange, for these plants like sun. Red

clover and every shade of blue cornflower could form a riotous meadow beneath. Even just a dusting of wild flowers will bring late-spring to summer colour to the trees and will provide contentment for birds, bees and butterflies.

A grove of trees will always create its own ambient style. Silver elegance can be provided with the fine-leafed ornamental pear, *Pyrus salicifolia* 'Pendula', sparsely placed, with a canopy filmy enough to allow lavender to be naturalised beneath. Perhaps with a path outlined in lavender-blue *Iris* 'Pacific Mist' to dissect the grove. But the soil must be gravelly and well drained, for the surface plants do not like damp roots. Where I have placed this collection, the ground has been gently sloped for natural run-off. Of course if olives can be grown, they would be a natural accompaniment.

The splendour of red, in both bark and leaf, above a floor of rocks, smooth stones and water in a landscape populated by maples suggests Eastern style: *Acer palmatum* is all autumn fire and *A. p.* 'Atropurpureum' a rich purple; *A. buergerianum* has orange-brown bark, while *A. davidii*'s brilliant orange shoots are optimum flames. Maples come as large trees or small shrubs, and varieties can be purchased that have been grown to weep and spread at different heights so a path or

stream can be swept by clouds of fine leaves. Never a purist, I'd carpet beneath the trees with Gucci-pink *Cyclamen neapolitanum* for autumn and *C. coum* in spring, to make a shocking coloured carpet, and in the clearings the unreal red grass *Imperata cylindrica* 'Red Baron' would hide rocky edges, making this naturalised planting one of gardening's most brilliant statements above and below. For the suggestion of a gate I'd place two lacquer-red poles in a focal position, just to create more striking colour.

It is generally accepted that space is needed to grow a grove of trees and that it is a delight that some urban dwellers must forgo. But this riot of small trees above tiny pink flowers could light any courtyard or balcony. Maples are excellent plants, their fine leaves naturally softening any surrounding hard surface. Nothing is more limited than space in urban Japan, but beyond many a gate a tiny area hosts these trees in pots, making a miniature woodland in one of the world's most populous spots.

Similarly, *Salix caprea* 'Kilmarnock', the dwarf pussy willow, parasol-shaped and covered with fur catkins in spring and fine foliage in summer, grows well in pots, and were it to be surrounded by pots of bulbs, all the beauty of a European wood in spring could be reinterpreted in a cool city courtyard.

Shrubs. I hear the word and a quiet feeling of boredom creeps over me. I see the rounded bushes in single file lined up against the neighbour's fence, kept trimmed annually, just high enough to hide it from view; one each of a favoured flowering variety, mostly with dull leaves after a single glorious burst of flower. For eleven months they have zero colour or architectural impact; they are like the old sofa against the wall – useful, undemanding and a comfortable background for more stirring elements.

philadelphus. That they remain in my garden till they flower in late spring is a yearly miracle, for their spindly, awkward, bare branches look dead while the rest of the garden has already come into flower and leaf. But when their arching canes laden with fragrant white blooms form a bridal tunnel across the path. I wonder why there are not more of them, and any sins are forgiven.

Philadelphus 'Virginal' is embarrassingly floriferous and perfumed, growing to 3m (10ft). *Philadelphus* x *lemoinei* is another

shrubs

But this image is really unfair, for shrubs placed or pruned imaginatively make the most spectacular gardens. They also provide form for mixed borders, and banked together they can make the hedges that provide bones for the garden. If space permits, one of the most dramatic ways to show off shrubs is by grouping one species together.

Some years ago I saw my first serpentine border, with intoxicatingly perfumed shrubs planted close together, to be spied from the snaking path through arches of clipped cypress on either side. The bushes were

scented variety, but not so tall, and *P.* 'Frosty Morn' has double flowers and a sweeter scent.

Philadelphus tolerate poor soils, cold and dry spells, but they must be pruned annually to control their shape. To provide some early structure I have placed them behind knee-high hedges of evergreen camellias, the single, white, scented *Camellia sasanqua*. Then, as the tunnel starts to take on the dull green of mid summer, *Hydrangea arborescens* 'Grandiflora' sends out cones, their points covered with dense heads of small, compact white flowers. I like

the icy green–white of *H. paniculata* 'Greenspire', which seems luminous in dappled shade. Grown on shaded banks or in pots to highlight a quiet corner, hydrangeas will withstand hot spells as long as they receive regular good drinks of water, and are among summer's most useful plants.

I fill the curves of sweeping parterres made from clipped dark green box or *Ilex crenata* 'Convexa', a small-leafed holly, with dwarf varieties of hydrangea that are mounds of lacy flowers – a charming summer combination. *Hydrangea serrata* var. *thunbergii* is a small-growing lacecap with pale blue rings of simple flowers around a boss of miniature flowers that look like crunched-up buds.

For sheer fantasy, hydrangeas grafted on to slender stems are so full of flower that they resemble extravagant powder puffs found in the expensive-looking boxes that graced Grandmama's dressing table. Growing through a low hedge, randomly punctuating a parterre or as tubbed sentinels, they bloom as the garden slips into its deep green phase.

Mahonia 'Apollo' *flowers and fruits in the darkest days of winter, but its evergreen leaves are always shiny, branching out in formation like giant bouquets.*

Weigela is another deciduous shrub that is just a mass of fine twigs until mid spring. These I now grow only as shapes, either rounded like exercise balls or as standard pompons.

The foliage of *Weigela florida alba* 'Alexandra', so deep and bronze as it backs flowers of mid pink, provides dramatic colour and architectural shape against perennials of mauve, purples and inky hues; while a double line of bright red-flowering *W.* 'Lucifer' as standard pompons makes an important entrance either side of a path. Its colour is anticipated with an underplanting of multi-flowered *Tulipa* 'Red Georgette' pushing through matching cardinal-red *Bellis perennis*, to make very vivid style in a still-wintering garden.

Until its lanky outstretched arms are lightly covered with long grey-green leaves, its tips encased with flowers, buddleia for me has very little to recommend it architecturally. But grown *en masse* beside a wall, in tones blending from dull white or blue to mauve pink and the deepest purple of *Buddleja davidii* 'Black Knight', attended by the omnipresent butterflies with the remnants of field grasses and flowers at their feet, this shrub makes one of the most atmospheric divides between the formal and the wild garden.

These plants need space, as new shoots can be 2m (6ft 6in) long each

summer. I tried containing their late-summer exuberance behind tall skeletons of toning grey cardoons, but after the inevitable summer storms they both became very wayward and had to be cut back.

At this season my garden needs these rounded spear-shaped flowers, so when I saw buddleia made into a formal shape I abandoned the tangled bushes and introduced the grafted standard pompons of blue flower spikes into the main border. *B.* 'Nanho Blue' now formed striking design and colour, flowering above the wiry form of the perennial *Eryngium alpinum* 'Blue Star'. Small shrubs of *Hebe* 'Amy' clipped as balls repeated the major

LEFT & RIGHT *Brilliant red Weigela in the potager at West Green House is clipped to make pompon trees that flower in early summer, giving form and shape to what are basically untidy shrubs.*

shrubs' colour and shape, and into this ocean of blue I encouraged a prostrate ceanothus, *C. thyrsiflorus* var. *repens*, covered with rich blue flowers, to creep over the bed's retaining wall.

Grey balls of cistus, covered with sun-loving, crepe flowers, and *Potentilla fruticosa* 'Abbotswood', also with single rose-shaped blooms, offered foils of white against dense small-growing shrubs to highlight the blue. All these plants like the same conditions, well-drained soils and warmth, but are hardy for more temperate zones too.

The ground carpeted in the grey-white furred leaves of *Stachys lanata* 'Silver Carpet' stopped the rounded shapes from becoming boring, and the two-toned blue *Muscari latifolium* introduced small, nearly pre-spring spikes to be followed by a bicolour blue Dutch iris 'Sapphire Beauty'. Altogether a traditional shrub bed had become the smart colour and form we appreciate in blue and white china.

As the light hangs low in the sky the shrubs can illuminate the season. Firelight colour in berry-covered shrubs brings late-season glamour when trained on buildings. The translucent berry skin collects every last ray of sun, and these hardy plants, now covered in orange or yellow or red, will hold their brilliant display from September to December in the northern hemisphere. Birds permitting.

I like the sheen of pyracantha's autumn berries, the thick clusters of white flowers in spring, and summer's deep green polished leaves. Easily grown and trained, it does need clipping to maintain its denseness. Pyracanthas flower from old wood, so even after quite ruthless pruning, they will flower and fruit beautifully.

The red-berried cotoneaster is less work; the *horizontalis* types fan naturally on to the walls and then need to be only lightly fixed. With dull leaves, cotoneaster is one of those plants that will grow nearly everywhere from drought-prone plains to shady temperate gardens, thriving on most soils and surviving lack of water and even gloomy cool light.

But as the last pre-winter berry is stripped away, the large whorls of spiky evergreen leaves of the mahonia are about to send forth clusters of clear yellow flowers that smell of honey in the cold winter air. Absolutely the one shrub that I adore, it looks perfectly composed free-standing in large clumps or on woodland floors. With hands completely leather-gauntleted, one perfectly rounded spray of cut leaves can be gathered to complete the Christmas flower arrangements in a northern-hemisphere drawing room.

Carefully chosen, there are varieties that will give flowers for the entire length of the winter season. *Mahonia aquifolium* 'Apollo' has blue-black berries behind the golden flowers, while *M. japonica* produces leaves of autumn tones. I look across it at the grotesquely contorted corkscrew hazel, *Corylus avellana* 'Contorta', its tiny branches arthritic and beautiful holding slender lime-yellow catkins, and I wonder why we bother with spring and summer and their overabundance of flowers, for these deep-winter shrubs give perhaps the best garden style.

But if garden style is our aim, a garden without shrubs cannot even be considered. Nearly every form or shape we make started life as a bush. The box we edge, hedge, shape and draw our paths with is a shrub, as are most hollies that can be used this way to make our background designs.

Viburnum tinus, which forms dense hedges, and *Ligustrum ovalifolium*, the green privet, have varieties with green and marbled leaves, and *Ligustrum delavayanum* has dense small leaves, making it another excellent plant to give architectural form.

We create design by planting the shrubs tightly in groups, or taking one to form a dramatic shape as it matures.

In fact, so many of the gardens we travel the world to see consist of thousands of green shrubs used as paintbrush strokes or textured mounds to produce a desired design.

What is a romantic garden? I find a cottage garden in early summer with its traditional riot of flowers and delicious scents utterly romantic. One afternoon in France I looked down on a long stretch of water, outlined by lawns and hedges, overhung by ancient avenues, where one white swan glided on its mirror surface; this too was serenely romantic.

Then I stood by one of the world's most exceptional herbaceous borders, an Irish master plantsman's design in lavenders, blues and mauves, and

urns, statues, follies, waterfalls and even the cavalier King Charles spaniels. I too have a lonely swan on a classically sylvan lake (I think the swan has had a 'domestic' – its partner simply walked away and wouldn't come home), so romance pervades my garden in all its guises.

But romance treads a fine line between glamour and kitsch. The solution, I believe, is in boldness in controlled design, in a careful choice of colour and in the selection of plants. The English climate allows for sensual

A very ordinary Australian dam has been planted to make a romantic lake bordered by mostly pink flowers. Delicate pink Iris 'Beverly Sills' and sways of predominantly

gardens with romantic themes

heritage roses are gradually spreading to cover the bank. Here Rosa 'Constance Spry', a David Austin bloom of cupped sugar pink petals, flowers in late October.

sighed, 'Oh, how romantic,' as I gazed at cascades of flowers, to be told, 'Yes, it's very 1980s.'

How can romance be outdated? Is it equated with the traditional romantic hero, the cavalier with a periwig and red-feathered hat, which would now be socially embarrassing? Perhaps, but I still crave the flamboyance and lost elegance he represents.

My own gardens give me away as an incurable romantic, borders prodigious with flower, alive with water, hedged and decorated with all the expected accoutrements – birds,

gardens that can form dangerous liaisons with reality, culminating in romantic perennial borders that entrance in the abundance of their seasonal beauty, but if we look beneath this floral lavishness, we see that they are held together by the most rigid garden design, the voluptuous effortlessness controlled every inch of the way.

Similarly, the seventeenth-century Dutch painters created breathtaking still-life masterpieces that were concepts of seasonally improbable bowls of fruit and flowers, yet these stunning compositions were all balanced within the confines of a

series of imaginary triangles. Working with the same principle, a garden designer can create an interconnecting series of pictures to control a collection of irrepressible plants, each vying to command attention.

My design would commence with bold plants, a choice of the leviathans of the perennial world, which would give the design importance and prevent the plan from descending into genteel prettiness. Romance requires a feeling of saturation, so planting should be bold, even quite provocative: beds should not be meanly planted. Into the centre of my conceptualised triangle I'd place giant tree peonies – for their flowers are huge grandfather cups of silken petals in spring – growing them in large tubs, as they are often seen in Chinese courtyards. Here I'd place

them on raised plinths, for tree peonies nearly always hang their heads too shyly for us to see; when they're displayed this way, their beauty is easily revealed and their grandeur enhanced. If space allowed, I'd place a group of four at differing heights, the bottom and shortest one the widest.

I'd choose the giant-size white petals of *Paeonia suffruticosa* 'King of White Lions', a tree peony whose base is smeared with purple, or the perfumed *P.* 'Kamadas Wisteria', with crumpled petals in rapturous lavender pink, or perhaps the mahogany dark *P.* 'Black Panther', which is quite low-growing and has a double flower nearly too large to form the base of my composition.

Lavish herbaceous peonies, all inward curving like oversized brandy balloons, are grouped below to continue my spring theme of extravagant blooms – the creamy white *Paeonia lactiflora* 'Florence Ellis' and the old variety *P. l.* 'Duchesse de Nemours'. The singular white peonies 'Lotus Queen' and 'Jan van Leeuwen' are also definitely first choices.

These are planted alongside groups of the tissue-paper oriental poppies, as large as coffee bowls, that are totally astonishing one-day wonders during their brief season. *Papaver orientale* 'Lilac Girl' has all the subtle mood that lilac can give and it does not scorch or

fade in direct sun as the exceptionally favoured plum-coloured *P. o.* 'Patty's Plum' seems to do. It is wise to plant poppies deep in the beds so that the large gaps they leave early in the season are less noticeable. Not all garden beds are viewed from one side, in which case these poppies are for the bed's centre.

The major flowers in my spring design are all round moon shapes, which I'd echo later in the season with the opalescent faces of white dahlias: the cactus-shaped *Dahlia* 'Baret Joy', which has 20cm (8in) rays of white light, whilst *D.* 'Vera's Elma' is a perfect globe. Dahlias are solid, staked and stiff plants to which I like to try and give an ethereal effect by grouping clumps of the whispering grass *Dierama* 'Guinevere' in front. I imagine the

effect to be of moons rising above an arching grass, hung with tiny white nightcaps at the path side, for this plant must have dry toes.

Once every few years in cool temperate gardens, a mammoth autumn flower evades the frosts and blooms over 3m (10ft) tall into the sky, cloaked in star-shaped lavender blooms. *Dahlia imperialis* is one of nature's most compliant plants, enduring seasonal tribulations of neglect and drought, dormant until well into summer, when it emerges to dice with the first frosts.

Stars must be included in a moon garden, and silver ones on strong sprays come as *Eryngium giganteum* flowering behind at summer's height, and rods of *Actaea matsumurae* 'White Pearl', a variety of this perennial autumn plant I've found easy to establish. *Actaea simplex* 'Brunette' is to be coveted, as it towers 2m (6ft 6in) tall with dark polished leaves and stems studded by nearly white flowers.

Late-summer nets of lavender-blue perovskia drift from behind, again closely cloaking the formal dahlias. Here, many plants planted like clouds of tulle become a bold statement in their own right. All smaller plants will create bold effects if handled this way, especially *Lysimachia clethroides*, creating lines of white curves as its head bends like the swan on the nearby lake.

Starched linear design in green and white is *Salvia* var. *turkestanica* 'Alba', which bridges high season; a statuesque annual plant with bracts as crisp as an Elizabethan gallant's linen.

Into these dreamy colours I'd introduce shades of the evil queen. The hooded chocolate-brown bonnets of *Aquilegia viridiflora* with bright yellow anthers have colour to remind me of the new season's return from the underworld. It looms above the early ground cover *Persicaria microcephala* 'Red Dragon', whose pointed leaves have rings of dark. Soon the wilful *Papaver somniferum* 'Black Peony', as rebellious and shiny as a satin-G-string wearer, walks on an early summer's wild side, never appearing in the same place twice.

To exaggerate these groups and multiply the beauty of these extravagant flowers, a strong architectural element, a triangular 2m (6ft 6in) cone, covered with mirror or polished steel, would reflect again and again the ever changing swish of the surrounding flowering skirts whilst firmly anchoring the tall drifts of flower. A single mirrored pyramid will suffice if that is all the space will allow, placed right behind the tallest peony; but repeated, it would create a hall of mirrors in a garden bed.

Water is perhaps the most romantic element. Inevitably the venerated

visions of Monet's delicate wisteria bridge suspended above a pond of floating water lilies at Giverny, the soaring fountains of the Villa d'Este at Tivoli, or the seventeenth-century baroque island garden in Lake Maggiore in northern Italy, cross the mind. But controlled and sophisticated use of water in a contemporary garden can introduce quite unique charm.

In the English city of Bath, historic terraced houses now listed with World Heritage cling to nearly vertical hills, some so dizzyingly steep that a romantic heroine would have had vertigo as she descended the steps. Here in a new garden of nearly impossible proportion, just 7m (22ft) across and 27m (90ft) long, and falling down 7m (22ft), a series of flat grass terraces are connected by central steps that are broken by an enchanting narrow water rill falling down the entire garden. This stream of water entices and connects the garden by the play of light on the slow-moving water ribbon, in a concept reminiscent of a Mogul garden, as the miniature stream glides and falls again and again, disappearing under clumps of aromatic lavenders, nepeta, salvias and blue cranesbill geraniums, until it rests in a small pond below. Each terrace mirrors the other, further controlling the design in an interplay of repeated pattern, making a geometric and

ABOVE *The romantic Stuart cavalier always seemed to pose with a Cavalier King Charles spaniel at his feet. This is a proud descendant, the divine Henrietta, recently departed.*

BELOW *Romantic pastoral figures seem to belong in romantic, flower-filled gardens.*

harmonious complement to the elegant proportion of the classic Georgian terraced house above.

A central canal reflecting an avenue of trees, the great château in the distance, must be one of gardening's most romantic concepts, an impossible dream – as romance always tends to be. But this delightful image translates superbly into town gardens, for the majority are awkwardly long rectangles.

A canal reduced to the desired length is an exemplary solution to maximise light and movement in a confined space and to add glamour to what could be a humdrum backyard. Of course Helen Dillon's Dublin city garden could never deserve that title, as it is this passionate plantswoman's *pièce de resistance*. However, with the advent

of the long canal stretching nearly the entire garden's length, an already extremely good garden has reached dizzying heights.

The canal replaces a rectangular lawn, which was always perfect, green and high-maintenance, but now, silvered water mirrors the blowzy summer plants on either side and the hard stone edging permits designs with pots filled with strong shapes and colour. Unexpectedly, Tasmanian dianella comes from the greenhouse as frosts depart and by mid summer its long dull green leaves are nearly obliterated by sprays of deep purple berries – perhaps an out-of-character plant for the traditional romantic vision of canal, garden and period house.

Water and trees alone can be enough to create a fascinating garden, especially where water is desirable to cool the air. Here, the geometric grid is paved in coral stone, with four square wells let into the surface, each alive with central bubbling fountains. Height was achieved by a pergola that cut the garden in four linear grid lines, its base clogged with exuberant plants, including the immense trumpets of *Brugmansia* x *candida*, the wine palm *Butia capitata*, with arched grey-green branches in contrast to the brilliant green of *Licuala*, the fan palm. Ferns and cordylines soften hard edging, while *Beaumontia grandiflora*, the pure white trumpet flower, is such a vigorous

Laughingly, Helen told me, 'I think the young gardeners accept this new design best,' but for me it illustrates perfectly how a normal suburban back yard can be turned into a space of great design and beauty.

vine, it absolutely tests the strength of the decorative pergola, where it is intertwined with the redolence of the wax-white flowers of *Stephanotis floribunda* to become the hypnotic essence of the South Seas.

The linear shape of the modern urban house and land simply enhances water and plants controlled within such a geometric design. Perhaps not traditional romantic concepts – but vogue glamour in courtyards and forecourts where sharp-edged ponds are superimposed with grids of planters placed as islands in perfect formation, filled with plant materials as diverse as stands of bamboo, iris and arum lilies grown as cubes, or chequerboards of clipped box.

LEFT *Modern sculptures overlook a mixed flower garden in Connecticut in which US landscape designer Dan Kiley has used wild plants from the American prairies.*

RIGHT *At Gresgarth Hall in Lancashire, English designer Arabella Lennox-Boyd's meadows become marginal plantings beside the lake. Native orchids flourish in this cool climate.*

Romance for many is a wild thing: a field or meadow sown with cornfield annuals of poppies, cornflowers and corncockles beneath an orchard of mature fruit trees. But like all good romances a lot of hard work underlies the artless result. In fact meadows are the most expensive and exasperating type of gardening I know. Soils must be treated to lose their fertility or topsoil scraped away, often ruthlessly by a bobcat. The wild-flower meadow mix must be of flowers known to suit the exact locality, and even the most desirable birds and gentle wind insist on infecting the soil with thistles or rye grass, which must be eradicated annually, often only by hand if you are to be truly successful.

For the flowers to continue to bloom abundantly it is wise to cultivate a portion of the field each year and replant it, as happens with agricultural land, or cheat as I do and heel in many of last year's corms and bulbs – generally anemones, ranunculi and tulips – for in time they will revert to become the simplest flowers in the following year.

But before the romance of the flowering mead engulfs the senses, it's wise to remember that before the season is warm enough to enjoy relaxing outdoors, this swathe of flowers will have died and what remains will be an area of rank brown grass. It requires the toughest machine to mow it three times at least before a green grass cover will return beneath the trees. Consider carefully whether such a fleeting two months of romantic beauty is all that you want from a garden.

Romance can also be the simplest of gestures: a single rose held in a garden statue's hand, petals tossed on the water of a birdbath. But romance can die if emotions go out of control; in fact a farce is played out when there are too many romantic ideas, especially in a garden where space is limited. One large urn richly planted or one arbour covered with the largest rose is charming, but too many multiples are not. Statues should be introduced to

birth control, and sculptures that are a flock of inanimate animals seem better hidden among grass and trees.

I often feel repetition looks best in simple forms: perhaps a long line of flowering Japanese cherries or a row of good pots with severely clipped bushes or trees – but every rule is there to be broken and often excess truly succeeds. Remember though that too many romances conducted at once lead to complications!

My latest romantic concept concerns just a tree, an old pin oak with sturdy low branches well pruned to let soft light slant down below. Last summer I started to collect old birdcages, twenty so far, all in different shapes and designs, each quite large enough for one brilliant golden canary to sing in happily all day long. These ornamental homes are hung at different levels throughout the lower branches, perhaps suggesting flowers among the dense leaves. A wooden ladder against the trunk is an Arcadian touch, allowing for practical maintenance, while white Versailles pots of azaleas in spring, then marguerites in summer, encircle the tree.

As winter approaches, the birds return to a practical aviary with hotel comforts, to dream I'm sure of returning to the enchanted tree next spring. I would like my traditional European cavalier to join me beneath the singing tree. I think he'd approve of this conceit, for he too knows that romance is an abstract idea that transcends every culture we impose on it.

a romantic cottage garden

In the spring of 2001 I was able to purchase the old village store along the road from my garden at Kennerton Green. Although derelict for years it still had the typical Australian nineteenth-century-style corrugated-iron veranda supported by wooden posts, with the central door and window either side that are synonymous with colonial buildings. Always, a few scraggy trees to which a horse and buggy could have been tied shaded these simple buildings, and neglected shrubs obliterated the front.

Cleared, the inevitable straight path from door to gate, edged in old bricks, reappeared to be gravelled in really white stone, with a post-and-rail fence and picket gate all painted bright white, maintaining the traditional hard landscaping. Now for the first time I had a suitable area to plant a cottage

June in England is pure floral romance. Roses tumble from walls and join tall perennials behind low borders of box. Even the painted period seat emphasises the traditional appeal of this style of gardening.

MARYLYN ABBOTT'S THOUGHTS ON GARDEN DESIGN

Many people believe that the cottage-garden look is the most romantic style of gardening. Here, many of the accoutrements we sigh over – arches laden with roses and honeysuckle, a flower-encrusted path leading to a picket gate – perfectly illustrate the ideal.

garden, a romanticised gardening concept that is still a delight to many gardeners.

Perhaps not a true cottage garden but a stylised approach, for only three plants associated with this style of garden were chosen – lilac, roses and lavender – to fill the 2.5m (8ft) square beds either side, now beginning to be hidden from the road by a hedge of *Syringa vulgaris* 'Katherine Havemeyer', the darkest of purple lilacs.

The two beds were planted thickly with the low-growing *Lavandula stoechas* clipped to make a 1m (3ft) high lavender lawn, its flower reminiscent of a deep purple bumble-bee topped by lavender-pink rotor petals which become host to this buzzing community. But soon I decided to make a pattern in each

bed with four rays radiating out from the centre, adding the white *L. stoechas* f. *leucantha* to make two rays. Both these lavenders grow to a companion height, so a flat pattern was again achieved. The brick edges on either side are now defined by a hedge of *L. s.* 'Willow Vale' and the flat-faced lavender rose 'Symphony in Blue', both growing to 75cm (30in) and planted not more than 45cm (18in) apart, with a blue cranesbill, *Geranium wallichianum* 'Buxton's Variety', poised to tie it all together. The remaining two sides and the veranda have become completely draped in the heritage rose 'Veilchenblau', all bunches of tiny faded-lavender flowers with coin-spot white eyes.

Bright colour was introduced by terracotta tubs with standard, clipped

kumquats, covered for months on end with miniature tangerine fruits. In cooler areas, the tiny lilac-mauve flowers of lilac 'Meyeri Palibin' would introduce a soft colour in mid spring; another choice would be a bright lollipop of *Lonicera serotina* 'Honeybush', a rich mid-purple honeysuckle, synonymous with cottage gardens.

The design is extremely simple, low-maintenance and water-efficient, and would, I feel, look fetching in a well-drained and sunny urban courtyard where the smaller space would capture the fragrances of each group of plants, flowering successively for approximately three months.

Just as the diaphanous drape adds more allure to the nude form, so do plants that form curtains and veils give a feeling of mystery to a garden. A view glimpsed through trees is more tantalising than a full frontal view from a plate-glass window, and thankfully a garden disaster can be softened by the introduction of quick-growing diaphanous plants to put up a translucent screen that will mask any faults.

Think of the beauty of the English countryside in May where through a

highways and byways and become very smart introductions into our gardens, promoted by the most respected plant collector Jamie Compton and nurserywoman Marina Christopher.

Many are self-seeding annual and biennial plants – architectural silhouettes with long arms holding aloft shallow plates of tiny flowers, which in winter become frosted garden sculptures, creating cobwebs of filmy beauty. These plants lift a complacently beautiful flower border on to another level of design.

veiled glory

mist of white lace flowers, the spikes of bluebells and the new green in hedges and bushes are seen covered by ravishing cow parsley – erroneously, I feel, regarded as a weed, for it is a member of the umbellifer plant family that can supply some of the most glorious natural planting devised this side of heaven. Today many of the umbellifer species have left the

Dahlias are often described as stiff, harsh plants, but veiled in grasses this marigold Dahlia 'Gaiety' is softened to become enmeshed in the garden design.

I grow a burgundy and clotted-cream tulip, *Tulipa* 'Gavota', through the fine mahogany leaves of a family member, the black cow parsley *Anthriscus sylvestris* 'Ravenswing', that seeds in both my gardens between paths and paving stones alike. With the shining red wallflowers 'Blood Red', then *Aquilegia vulgaris stellata* 'Ruby Port', they provide strong colour not usually associated with spring.

The umbellifer *Angelica sylvestris* 'Vicar's Mead', a dusty pink flower above deep ferny leaves is viewed through the skeletal thistle *Cirsium rivulare* 'Atropurpureum', whose flowers of intense magenta create a glow around this moody group. *Cirsium* is a pernickety plant, loathing competition; it must be a border screen where it will perform happily in self-imposed isolation, framing a story beyond.

As the border turns from mauves to purples in the walled garden at West Green House, an entire corner is misted by 120cm (4ft) high twiggy stems of hardy and uncomplaining umbellifers that look like mist. Amethyst *Thalictrum aquilegifolium* appears first, then *T. delavayi* 'Hewitt's Double' takes its place at summer's height. They firstly ensure a frame for spring's lavender-blue *Lupinus aridus* 'Summer', then form tracery patterns for *Salvia verticillata* 'Purple Rain', a totally saturated collection of deep purple rosettes on matching stems. As I walk towards the northern end of the walled garden, I believe I hear the grand strains of Mendelssohn in a three-month recital, as plants here are swathed in a continuous wedding veil of tiny flowers.

Like the dotted net of an expensive hat, *Thalictrum aquilegiifolium* 'Album' has spots of white fluff on its fine foliage, and London's Brompton Oratory itself is challenged in grandeur by clouds of *Crambe cordifolia*. The dramatic stalks of 2m (6ft 6in) sprays, studded by tiny white flowers on

Hopeless in Australia, where it just looks washed out, the smoky blue delphinium, D. 'Gillian Dallas', adds soft, atmospheric colour to a steel border in countries where the light is less bright, and is a perfect foil for harsher shapes such as cardoons and echiums.

spider-thin twigs, are a spectacle that is followed by *Gypsophila paniculata* 'Bristol Fairy', which are simply gossamer flowers.

The white flower-encrusted points of spring-flowering *Eremurus* 'Brutus', then self-seeding curtains of *Linaria purpurea* 'Alba' could be termed the rods of a chancel screen, continuing the ecclesiastical theme.

Garden fashion decrees that transparent grasses are essential to the beauty of the herbaceous border. Perhaps so, but grasses for me are at their majestic best as plantings in awe-inspiring groups of hundreds of identical plants that can catch the wind and form great windswept patterns or trap the wind's ghostly noises.

Grasses do stop solid plants from becoming too dominant, whilst these

in turn anchor the wispy leaves, each creating blocks of colour and texture, excellent as a repeated pattern. I remember a double border at Glyndebourne in East Sussex, where golden August evening light lit the tall seed heads of *Stipa gigantea* as it broke the formal planting, creating all around it an ethereal haze.

A garden without many levels of height becomes just a flat sea of colour, but tall swags or drapes of vines or plants pull the eye up and around, sometimes to frame the light or to highlight a plant.

Rampant summer vines can create nearly instant curtains. The curious lavender and cream *Phaseolus caracalla*, the snail vine, is fun to grow and its seeds are available in many catalogues. A self-seeding vine in warmer climates, it can cover a fern house or an arch during the hottest months, ready to be taken down to open the garden up when winter light is needed.

Think of creating a draped shawl of letterbox-red-flowered *Tropaeolum* over a dull summer-green hedge, or allow the golden hop *Humulus lupulus* 'Aureus' to screen the summer outdoor eating area from neighbouring eyes. Hops dry so well and when they are taken down at season's end they look superb tied to rafters and falling from kitchen dressers and cupboards to make interior curtains.

Is there a cool temperate garden without the most romantic curtain combination – a climbing rose intertwined with clematis? The sheer thought of the green and white *Clematis* x *diversifolia* 'Duchess of Edinburgh' trailing through a favourite old climbing rose like *R.* 'Mrs Herbert Stevens' – a white tea rose tinged in green and heavy with fragrance – is a vision of pure garden glamour. Or the deep purple-blue *Clematis* 'The President' clinging to *Rosa* 'Charles de Mills', a large crimson gallica that easily covers a garden tripod.

Two species of clematis I've found that accept the harsher conditions are *C. armandii*, just strands of almond-pink blossom with long, dull leathery leaves, and the white *C. montana alba*.

Parasol frames allow wisterias to form giant curtains, veiling part of the garden at Nahroo, west of Sydney.

They are both tough vines, withstanding 100°C heat and English snow. Within two years they will have a pergola under control, even to be classed as thugs, but schooled and trained they are exquisite single flowers that are happy to grow.

The most atmospheric curtained garden I know was created in the Blue Mountains west of Sydney by Dr Peter Valder, whose book *Wisterias* is a must-have reference book for all of us who wish to grow this magnificent vine. Confronted by the need for more space to place his vast collection of wisteria varieties, Peter turned his eyes to the rarely used family tennis court. He trained his vines up stands to resemble lace-edged umbrellas; they were then displayed in chequerboard fashion upon the grassed rectangle. It looked like a field from a medieval court of love – pavilions in shades of blue, lavender, mauve, pink and white, enabling the curious to part the tresses of flowers, inhale the heady aroma and enjoy the perfection.

When I came all those years ago to Kennerton Green, a huge *Wisteria sinensis*, a gift I believe from Peter, was already a giant mushroom held in shape by pillars of iron and stout chain. An eye-catching lavender extravaganza, it stood as the predominant feature in a garden space that already contained too many garden ideas – a white pool pavilion, a long border of pale camellias, the pool, a barbecue patio. It was desperate for a repeated planting pattern, so I turned to four pots of *W. sinensis*, repeating the shape of trained umbrellas and placing one at each of the pool's four corners. Repeating colour, repeating the same plant, is one of the most successful and simplest ways of creating pleasing garden designs.

Thanks to the work of Peter Valder and generations of plant collectors, we can choose from a range of wisteria colours. Nurseries standardise wisterias, and growers will graft standards, if ordered, or you can simply take a vine and train it around a stout steel frame to make a tall plant for border height. The violet-blue *W. floribunda* 'Violacea Plena' would shine among the shades of a purple plant collection and *W. floribunda* 'Magenta' is a pinky mauve which would add depth to a colour plan using a blend of pink to mauve.

Wisterias will keep their shape if the unwanted new tendrils are snipped back after flowering. But grow a wisteria just for perfume. Drape it across an arch that must be passed through each day, for it is among nature's most delicious sensual feasts for three weeks each year.

I think gardeners should apologise to annuals, for over the last century they have taken their bright flowers, grown for just a seasonal delight, and treated them like pâté goose, overbreeding, overfeeding and over-colouring them to such a degree that many of these once delicate field flowers are now gross and despised.

Beguiled by mass colour, gardeners have bored everyone by planting whole beds, generally round ones, with just one plant variety, often with a tonally disastrous fuchsia suspended in the centre.

was an annual. I now realise that after decades of bad press, gardeners do not even consider annuals when designing planting schemes, so unusual varieties are not now known.

Annuals in design will always be fleeting pictures, a divertimento to highlight an object or to build colour pictures, but at times they are absolutely essential. In early spring when first fronds are just pushing through it is only annuals that will chaperone the great bulb displays we yearn for after months of grey.

annuals

It is unfair to ask annuals to be a major design statement, for originally they were just bit players in a meadow chorus, and this is how they should remain in garden design. For me they are very important plants and I would not even consider planning a garden without them, as sown at regular intervals some varieties can provide kaleidoscope colour all year.

I did not realise how 'non-U' annuals have become in England. At first I was unnerved when correct lady gardeners looked pityingly at me when I told them the flower they admired

When designing an early-spring planting scheme, I rely on strong architectural objects to give coherence to plantings of bulbs and annuals that can become far too massed. In long lines that cross the entire garden, humble stakes are made into tripods in shades graded from fire-engine red to burgundy, with *Viola* 'Scarlet Red Shades' splashed at their feet like paint.

The annual Queen Anne's lace smothers hot pink Nicotiana *in the St Jean de Beauregard potager borders (see p. 127).*

Cosmos provides soft veils for a mid-summer garden. An easy-to-grow annual sown in early spring, it joyfully pushes through spent rose bushes and perennials, covering them with new flowers.

A toning wallflower and the goblet-shaped tulip *Tulipa* 'Old Tom' give a deep red glow to this hot planting in a cool-season garden.

The red stakes are crossed by more simple tripods to form a giant St Andrew's cross, now in shades from marigold to tangerine, supported by *Viola* 'Scarlet Orange' and a wallflower mix in apricot, cream and yellow with a hint of mauve called 'Glasnost'; beneath another peony-style tulip, 'Allegretto', all orange red with yellow tips. Borders planted exactly the same on either side are often referred to as mirror plantings, and here the garden design is repeated in stakes in shades of blue crossed by a line in grades of purple.

By late spring, sweet peas to match the stakes are a perfect plant –

exquisite perfume, a pea-shaped flower, stiff stems – and by a staggered planting their season can last well towards summer's end.

For exhibition and prizes they are perfect growing up no-nonsense strings or chicken wire, alongside sheds and fences or as alleyways. But for garden exuberance why not partner a speckled red sweet pea 'Raspberry Ripple' with a red and cream borlotti bean 'Lingua de Fuoco'?

I also plant sweet peas to hang down from tall pots or I weave them through small hazel border margins to create edges of brilliant flower. When they are planted this way the long stems are forfeited, but in late summer the plants are allowed to escape to trail across the path and form veils, an effect encouraged in my late-summer gardens.

Great banks of perennials have often reached vulgar proportions by mid summer, so strong design statements made by annuals need to be conspicuous to achieve some order.

A sturdy bold-leafed plant, *Ricinus communis* 'Carmencita', the castor oil plant, 2m (6ft) of deep-cut brown leaves and bright red spiky seed pods, is theatrical surrounded by slightly taller poles of fire-engine red topped with gold balls and draped by the sweet pea *Lathyrus* 'Firecrest'. When it's planted in late spring, the timber poles protect the new ricinus plant, then

enhance it when in deep summer it commands the border.

Or try curtaining the tall-growing white annual *Cosmos bipinnatus* 'Purity', which rises to 120cm (4ft), in large cylindrical-shaped rods of shiny flat aluminium. Together the fragile flower and its architectural support form a strong design to regiment a cool-colour flower bed. The spider flower, cleome, could achieve the same significance. Cleome is also available in soft pinks and magenta and even unsupported it grows well above tired plants, forming arms of softly fluid height.

For most of us annuals are garden accents in containers to bring exuberant colour to an entrance in early spring or to cascade from summer urns and take the eye away from perennials that are decidedly debilitated by now. I like to complement the tones of a container: in a terracotta pot, I think shades of salmon and blues foiled with limey white colours enhance and subdue the strong earth tones.

In spring I plant white and green *Euphorbia marginata* 'Summer Circle' below ice-white tulips, with brick-coloured *Diascia* 'Apricot Queen' to follow. For many, diascia is perennial, but I find it must be replanted annually. I mix it with *Antirrhinum* 'Jamaican Mist', all salmon sunset shades, and branches of the waxed rose tones of *Aeonium arboreum* 'Zwartkop', a glaucous plant that always gives rise to comment, and the pot reaches its apex at summer's end when the cream-marbled leaves of *Nasturtium* 'Jewel of Africa' tumble towards the ground, nearly obliterating the pots beneath.

Or fill a grey urn with the navy blue, aqua and grey green of *Cerinthe major* 'Purpurascens' together with the great round shape of the purple-blue cabbage 'Red Drum Head'. The soft grey leaves of *Dichondra* 'Silver Falls' with deep blue *Lobelia* 'Cascade' or *Verbena* 'Blue Lagoon' creeping out from the edges will hold its own in high summer. This could be preceded by *Brassica oleracea* 'Acephala', the flowering late-winter kale, marvellously frilled in shades from magenta to ice white, which needs cold nights to make the leaves colour. I particularly like the white kale 'Greenleaves' together with *Viola* 'White Perfection', a miniature flower with much charm.

Where summers are even warmer I create great bouquets in urns with chartreuse *Zinnia* 'Envy', green *Nicotiana alata* 'Lime Green' and round oak-leaf lettuce, with green amaranthus as the centrepiece – the weird swollen shapes of its seed arms never failing to fascinate.

As the summer zenith passes, many annuals are fey and floppy, so to contain them I often place three tall bamboo stakes equally spaced around a pot, then tie in a horizontal circle made of bamboo sticks, each one half as long as the measurement between each vertical stick, holding all together with raffia, just as expensive orchids are often presented in floral decorators' shops.

Then as autumn approaches, I plant gourds, small weird shapes in cream, green and yellow – some bottle shaped, others orange-, green- and cream-striped Turk's caps – to spill over the sides or to be trained up supports with golden green-eyed rudbeckia flowers. These miniature gourds need a wide trough or basket for they are rampant, but great fun to grow, harvest and keep until the following spring as household ornaments. By summer they start to disintegrate, but no jeweller could create such gems for display.

For centuries, meadow flowers and grasses have cohabited in harmonious drifts, helping to prevent unstable seaside cliff faces from eroding, holding sands together and providing colour carpeting beneath wind-tossed shrubs.

From a secluded beach north of Sydney, a path made from old weathered sleepers curves up the shallow cliff, a strong design line leading to a wide terrace made of the same slabs but now placed in bold herringbone pattern. The path is

Nasturtium 'Empress' and the sweet pea Lathyrus odoratus 'Wiltshire Ripple' are early-season climbing annuals that can give a look of informality to the garden.

bordered by parallel lines of old timber, decorated in between by handfuls of beach pebbles and shells.

Here there is no formal planting, just seeds scattered each year with handfuls of home-made mulch: simple flowers such as the blue felicia, with a golden eye and daisy shape, along with the native blue daisy, brachyscome, with quilled petals and fine creeping foliage. Both these plants grow well for me in England too (but here planted as seedlings). As if rolling the sea ashore these small blue flowers have embedded themselves among ornamental grasses of unthreatening height.

The perpetual motion of mature opalescent brown and new green pods among slender *Briza maxima* draws the eye up this cliff of nodding lanterns, a wild, magical sight. This 'shivering grass', as I knew it as a child, planted in well-defined swathes, can create powerful designs despite its apparent fragility.

The floating fur beige tails of *Lagurus ovatus* beside the frilled pincushion shape of *Scabiosa* 'Dusty Blue' is a satisfying blending of solid and cosmic form, especially appealing beside a path of slate-grey pebbles. Another plant that will be treated either as an annual or as a perennial, depending on the climate.

Hollyhocks love the seaside, where prevailing winds discourage the rust that makes them a problematical garden plant. They like it tough, reseeding between walls and paths – too much love will kill them. They look best planted in large clumps silhouetted against the sky, tall and majestic with flowers the texture of the best lingerie.

I believe beachside plantings should not overpower the grandeur of the majestic view beyond but harmonise tonally with the local environment. The garden can only complement an already glorious position.

But having said that, a cascade from doorside tubs of the navy-blue-eyed white osteospermum daisy – an annual in England but as tough as nails under the Australian sun and a perennial here – is part of a seaside summer, just as much as the unfortunate large white petunias that I now forgo, for they become pulp after heavy downpours.

'A world apart', by any definition, is the most romantic annual garden I know. It is at St Jean de Beauregard, near Paris. Here annuals are planted as huge borders around wide beds of mixed vegetables in a superb potager. A virtuoso performance of graded colours with flowers tightly packed to form saturated borders, one a tonal story in golds, then another in pinks and then lavender blues.

The golden border rises to tall sunflowers beside the wide green leaves of *Nicotiana sylvestris*, with its long white bells, and the large pompons of marigolds 25cm (20in) tall, with drifts of mid-size white cosmos and chirpy brown-striped French-style marigolds at their feet. Stiff green bells of Ireland, *Molucella laevis*; green tassels of *Amaranthus caudatus*; lime-green nicotianas and soft dahlias from gold to apricot spread out around wide vegetable gardens.

In the pink borders the green flowers are accompanied by shocking-pink nicotiana, cosmos and verbena, with drifts of white Queen Anne's lace, beside softer pink petunias, zinnias and snapdragons, and splashes of red-stemmed ruby chard. These justifiably famous borders are planted so that their maturity coincides with the harvesting of the vegetables and are stripped away along with the vegetables as the gates close on this seasonal garden.

In my student days, I lived in a very utilitarian block of red-brick flats, with a balcony exposed to blazing sun and winds that felt as if they came directly from the Antarctic Circle. On this inhospitable cantilevered block of cement I placed a row of cheap and cheerful glazed pots in citrus shades, in which I planted ordinary pot marigolds. The flowering season was short, just about six weeks after the long summer holidays, but their round smiling faces induced me to join them with a glass of cheap 'Château

A mixture of bulbs (Lilium 'Dark Beauty'), perennials (Coreopsis) and annuals (Atriplex hortensis var. rubra) in a midsummer bed at West Green House illustrates how interdependent all styles of plants are when it comes to making groupings of brilliant colour.

Cardboard' wine each evening, for the simple arrangement of colourful pots and flowers had made an avoided space welcoming.

Perhaps this is why we plant annuals in whatever space we have, for though we know their season is fleeting, their colours are an immediate joy and we can find an instant flower to suit every position.

Home vegetable gardens are not only fields of productivity, they are also compositions of notable leaves and flowers that form an integral part of the garden. The presentation of our culinary beds is as important as that of the herbaceous border. Just as we peruse cooking magazines to see the way inventive chefs display food, I believe productive garden design should be a pictorial reminder of how beautiful food plants are to grow, not just to eat.

To make these annual gardens the beds are rotovated and top dressed in and metal buckets brimming with the lavender and purple of chicory 'Palla Rossa' beside a washing tub of purple kohl rabi, its branches protruding like a space invader, would make sharp design and colour.

Parsley, chives, thyme, rosemary and basil all make aromatic table centres, and germinating seed bowls with colourful markers create an exciting corner for the curious.

Basil is an annual to be successively planted to ensure a continuous supply. Germinated in the greenhouse it is

the cook's garden

late winter. Any structures are built in spring, and the majority of seeds are sown *in situ* once the ground is warm enough.

Careful selection of plates and cutlery will culminate in a superb table arrangement; so too a selection of pots and baskets in which to grow the food ingredients can be arranged to make stunning style. Containers for growing vegetables can be as imaginative as you are. Place a display by the kitchen door, using the porch to support courgettes, cucumbers and trailing beans. Vegetables and herbs like to grow in pots, and a collection of silver

planted out once any suggestion of frost is over and the ground is warm. It absolutely hates wet seasons – even with good drainage it can drown in summer rains. The soil should be rich and very well drained. For continuous good leaves it is necessary to pinch out the emerging flowers. Basil plants adore warmth and are happy in pots in courtyards and on windowsills, where if treated with total respect they will grow right through into early winter.

A cook's garden must be many things: primarily a healthy organic patch with enough of a single planting to be productive; but it can also be a

garden of surprises and include a few special plants to make a dish more subtle or exotic.

❁ Wherever your kitchen garden grows, the soil must be rich in nutrients, for vegetables are greedy. Spread rotted manure or compost on the basic soil; then, as growth commences, I prefer a seaweed or fish-based liquid fertilizer.

❁ Compost heaps do not have to be the eyesore at the bottom of the garden. Strong woven panels can be used to make a giant garden basket for layers of leaves, stalks and grass clippings to be put in. Blood and bone and the herbs tansy and comfrey assist the rotting process. As the basket is filled, seasonal potatoes, melons or pumpkins can be grown on top. Then, at autumn's end, empty the basket of goodness on to the cleared vegetable patch or into pots and start the cycle again.

❁ Vegetables need regular watering, so a tap or hose nearby is vital, but best of all is an irrigation system laid to each bed.

Part of the oriental vegetable garden at West Green House (see p. 136). Bamboo pipes carried water which eventually emptied into a pebble pool feeding an underground irrigation system.

✂ Pests – snails, slugs, moths, caterpillars – are all waiting in the wings, so it's eternal vigilance. I don't like chemical sprays so I use a pyrethrum alternative and I try to plant a companion plant encircling the seedlings. Every visit to the garden I make is generally spent picking out by hand every slug or snail I spy. I'm always defeated and end up using slug pellets.

✂ Buy the basic seeds and seedlings locally from a neighbouring nursery; they will have climate-suitable varieties. Enjoy the international seed catalogues and try the seeds that appeal to see if they will grow in your area. But for more certain success, buy from growers as near as possible to your locality, for seeds selected by growers in Mediterranean areas are generally not for cool climates and vice versa.

✂ Wind is lethal to new seedlings and damaging to brittle vines, and whether the herbs, vegetables or fruit are in a garden or in pots, some form of wind-protection is essential. Espaliered fruit trees make my windbreak walls, but grape vines and roses together over fences is a delightful alternative. Stands of tall plants – corn, sunflowers, dahlias (firmly staked) – or tunnels made from bent saplings interwoven with cucumbers, courgettes, beans and small squash are breathtaking encircling a garden.

✂ Beds that are constantly being rotated need a decorative edge. Hedges of box or chives (but keep them looking trim) and rosemary are firm favourites, but seasonal plantings are captivating. Perhaps wide frills of parsley, with marigolds or calendula and compact nasturtiums, which are also a threat to aphids, between them. Small woven panels in hazel or willow, even boards painted in primary hues have great appeal. In Sweden I saw a careful gardener had encouraged his pumpkins to trail over a hard edge, manoeuvring each new pumpkin to rest on a straw nest on the pathway beside. It was folksy, charming and prevented the pumpkins' bases from rotting.

✂ Vines and tall plants require supports. From tripods of home-cut stakes to designer creations, they give the productive garden glamour. My vote for sheer exuberance must go to a straw scarecrow that had small squash plants trained up it and tied around the waistline so that the golden shapes hung like a hula skirt!

planting for cooking

The annual pleasure of designing intricate geometric patterns for my potager and discovering vegetables mainly for their shade and shape has long been ongoing. But it was on a visit to an exhibition garden in France that the ingredients for gazpacho, a traditional Spanish summer soup, triggered other thought patterns. Here the designers had placed the growing vegetables in silver olive-oil drums in a pool of water and paved the path in olive pips. The sheer exuberance of this recipe garden inspired the idea to plant the recipes that are used in the West Green House garden tearoom. So the long beds that bask in the reflected warmth along the garden's west walls had tall box hedges planted as buttresses to form bays for plantings that would be ravaged by daily harvesting.

In the traditional family potager the geometric pattern outlined by small clipped hedges keeps the garden neat, but here the plantings would have to be large. Harvesting just one leaf per lettuce or every second leek to keep the vegetable patterns intact in the traditional manner would give us nonsense quantities, so the design would have to incorporate

The lower terrace of the garden at the Château de Villandry, in the Loire area of France, houses the potager that has inspired the world's vegetable gardens since its inception in the first years of the twentieth century.

architectural elements to keep the area visually pleasing.

Giant woven baskets were made by a local craftsman from saplings in the woods to provide containers for the contents of vichyssoise, a soup of potatoes, leeks and onions, with the space in between the baskets filled with lavender-flowering chives that decorate the soup.

The ingredients for ratatouille, a Mediterranean vegetable dish, cannot be planted out until soils are warm and the temperature is rising, so the majority of the vegetables are started in the greenhouse in rows of terracotta pots, then placed out in radiating rays from potted bay and olive trees in the garden. Row upon row of tomatoes, peppers and aubergines, the pots removed once harvesting is complete. The lines of pots are separated by onions grown *in situ*.

Green-leaf vegetables look very moth-eaten after continuous harvesting and these plants bolt with warm days. So two long bays completely encased in gone-to-seed parsnips, with eye-high ferny leaves and flat umbellifer-shape lime flowers, give the leaves the privacy they need.

Instant rustic-looking hedges can be made by tying bundles of twigs together. The fine branches cut from dormant birch trees are just pushed into the ground, often at an angle. The twigs, caught together, become a line of instant trellis – a thrifty farmer's barricade that will support later tomatoes and other vines.

It is essential to plan for a continuous planting, starting with early-spring purslane and rocket and greenhouse-started lettuce. Plantings always include 'Kellys', a lettuce sown in November. It is essential that our salads look gorgeous so leaves in as many possible shades and textures are planted, from the near-black frills of 'Black Red' to the shaded leaves of 'Marvel of Four Seasons', now available in rotation for five months. I make lettuce-planting a small design exercise in colour, graduating the leaf colours in lines from soft green to black over the summer season. It's easy to do, as the catalogues give an over-abundant choice of varieties that will mature at different intervals.

a native american garden

In my quest for new plants and planting combinations I once met with a Native American, and sat in his potager beside the Potomac river in Maryland, USA. As I drove away past stalls brilliant with piles of orange jack-o'-lantern pumpkins and bunches of Indian corn, I decided I would like to interpret what I had seen around his tepee in my own garden the next season. I know I could have done without the woven hazel tepee and the canoe moored in a 'river' of sea-green kale in my English garden, but gardening is an experience of enjoyment and so these two symbols of indigenous America were enmeshed into the garden design.

The tepee was backed with six varieties of corn in lines, including 2m (6ft 6in) high 'Tuxedo', a sweet variety that withstands drier conditions; 'Dickson' for an early July crop; the purely decorative Indian corn; and the ornamental striped corn leaf 'Quadri'. In green, cream and pink, growing to 1.5m (5ft), it makes a dominant presence. I recommend growing it alone as a hedge or fence to create a seasonal bold plan.

Groups of the scarlet popcorn 'Red Strawberry', with 1cm (2in) cobs, flanked the tepee opening, and as the season concluded these tiny festive cobs, now harvested and piled up in decorative woven baskets, caught the late sun.

Sunflowers, in the coppery reds of *Helianthus* 'Velvet Queen' and the pure sulphur of 'Lemon Queen', stood among tripods of beans mostly selected from varieties offered in American seed catalogues.

Tomatoes, again grown in terracotta pots, came from the greenhouse: pink 'Grapefruit' with a yellow skin and pink flesh; 'Italian Gold', egg-shaped and orange; 'Green Grape', a medium-sized yellow green; and reliable red 'Moneymaker'.

Only a very warm summer encourages peppers to grow in Hampshire, so black 'Sweet Chocolate', scarlet red 'Beauty Bell' and yellow 'Lutyens' also started life in the sheltered warmth.

Amaranthus, an essential grain in the Native American diet, were planted for their outrageous height and shapes: *A. caudatus* 'Fatspike', with fat spider legs, and the tasselled *A.* 'Intense Purple'.

Through the tall vegetables and at the pathside were sown seeds of the

The miniature Helianthus *'Teddy Bear' amongst a meadow planting of prairie flowers, part of the design for the Native American potager at West Green House (below).*

American prairie flower and *Eschscholzia*, Californian poppy, in a mix of yellow, white and gold. Daisy-shaped *Coreopsis* and *Tithonia*, the Mexican sunflower, are both Inca treasure colours, and *Thunbergia*, the black-eyed Susan vine, in vanilla and orange scampered towards the path. The yellow of *Cosmos* 'Cosmic' and Thompson and Morgan's lupins in 'Yellow Shades' reminded me of escaped roadside colour seen on a drive to Whistler, north of Vancouver in Canada.

KEY

nicotiana

sunflowers

sunflower 'Teddy bear'

corn

red corn

prairie flowers

kale

tomatoes

peppers

echinacea

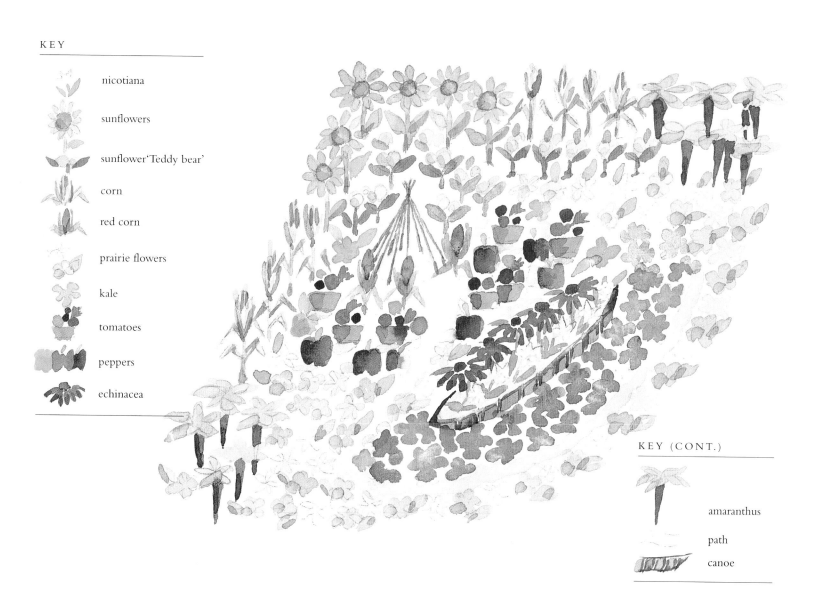

KEY (CONT.)

amaranthus

path

canoe

The canoe, woven from locally cut saplings, housed plants with known healing properties: *Echinacea pallida*, its flower often likened to a red head in a pink skirt; the tobacco plant, annual *Nicotiana* and tall *N. sylvestris*, 1m (40in) tall and hung with white tubular bells.

The absolute delight we, the gardening team, had in drawing this childish plan, sourcing, sowing, then planting out the different seed varieties and constructing our 'Indian' village, convinced us that we would indulge in another fantasy next year.

an oriental vegetable garden

The design inspiration for this garden was provided by the fields seen from the roads anywhere in South East Asia – the vegetables neat in rows, water

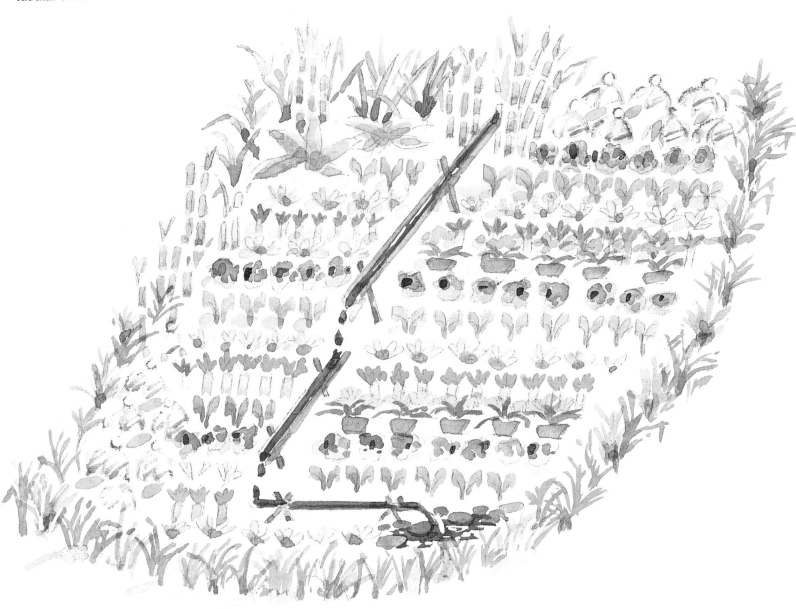

transported by bamboo irrigation pipes, the perimeter enclosed by grasses and a thicket of bamboo in a stand to one side.

To realise this oriental landscape the bed was raked smooth and water was laid to the garden with a pump and a return tank installed. Then the

KEY

giant red mustard

pak choy

Japanese parsley

leeks

lilies

basil in cloches

mixed grasses

miscanthus

bamboo

miniature bamboo

water in bamboo pipes

stones

scaffolding of tall bamboo to carry the water pipes that crossed the entire design at graduating heights was erected, with the water emptying into a pebble pond with a network of underground pipes.

From beneath the central water feature the green-leaf vegetables of Asian cuisine were planted in precise lines, exactly as they are by Asian farmers. Row upon row of shiny, soft, delicious green included:

✳ Flowering purple choy sum: coloured stems and leaves with flowers – all delicious when cooked.
✳ Mitsura or Japanese parsley: soft, long stems and heart-shaped leaves.
✳ Mizuna: fine green leaves for salad.
✳ Tatsoi or Rosetta pak choi: stiff plants with snow-white stems and wide green leaves for blanching.
✳ Chop-suey green shungiku or chrysanthemum greens: these are cooked like spinach but the leaves are far more aromatic.
✳ Wong bok: long cylindrical hearts of crisp green, finely pleated leaves.

Woven bamboo cloches allowed oriental coriander to trail through, and thin lines of elegant red and white

oriental shallots added long-leaf texture to a leafy design.

Flowers, as is oriental custom, were placed out seasonally in pots: tree peonies in spring; masses of lilies in June, July and August – Asiatic, oriental and tiger lilies in shades of creams and yellows; then chrysanthemums, tidy and stiff in the wildness of an autumn garden.

A second garden across the path was designed from a remembered courtyard in a family compound in the New Territories beyond Hong Kong. Here, a bonsai collection was displayed on bamboo benches of varying height, placed on crisply raked gravel. West Green House's head gardener, Dominic Rendell, had been for years carefully transplanting tree seedlings from the garden and woodlands and now his developing collection of bonsai trees became the garden showpiece.

Both gardens were then encased in grasses and bamboo. The tall and well-established bamboos were loaned from our local nursery, just tubs of the hardy bamboo *Fargesia murielae*. The grasses included: *Carex hachijoensis* 'Evergold', a low-growing variegated green and gold, its leaves as curling fingers; the fine yellow and green foliage of *Molinia caerulea* 'Variegata'; and *Pennisetum compressum*, a slender grass that gives small brown summer plumes. They provided decorative informality, a replica of the grss-filled ditches that outlined these beds of exactness in Asia.

To design and plant just those leaves used in one style of cooking is an unparalleled experience for a gardening cook. Watching from germination to harvesting teaches when leaves are best, which plants will grow back quickly, which will bolt; and by continual harvesting an understanding of the aromas and textures of the leaves is gained.

As leaf plants used in oriental cooking are quick-growing, just like our familiar salad vegetables, the designs must allow for successive sowings of one variety. The bare patches then become the home of the potted flowers.

a fragrant herb garden

Just as the gardens of Marrakesh influenced my paradise garden at Kennerton (see pp. 66–76), so they were the inspiration behind a seasonal herb garden at West Green House.

The lasting impression of Marrakesh was of fragrance and colour: the tiny horse-drawn carts brimming with small bunches of freshly picked sweet mint, which we purchased to make hot tea; the smell of roasted almonds at confectioners' doors; the pyramids of spices in the souks. Aromatic plants – rosemary, lavender, roses and scented geraniums – are grown in massed rows to be distilled into oils, and the hot evenings intensify the smells of coriander, fennel, cumin seed, parsley, sage and lemon thyme arising when the conical lid of the tagine is opened.

Walls of warm mud-pink, the deep blue and aqua in tiles – every sense was so beguiled that I came home determined to design an aromatic herb garden combining these colours and aromas at West Green House. The canals were to be outlined by wide sand edges decorated by rosettes of sempervivums, and would terminate at wide deep blue bowls where rose petals floated on cooling water.

Into the four square beds went mints – seventeen varieties, including rose, guava, lemon, nutmeg, apple, peppermint and ginger – and scented geraniums. To add height, tall stands of fine *Iris sibirica* 'Perry's Blue', the colour of sky, were grown for early blue flower, with blue agastaches continuing the height and colour into autumn. Coriander threaded through clouds of catmint, and curly green parsley contained the square design within an aromatic border.

In a semicircle, desert palms, loaned by our long-suffering nurseryman, and deeply perfumed roses in shades of old rose, all in pots, and dusty tamarisk trees gave height to this garden.

In the second garden bed across the path another curve of these plants backed a Persian-carpet design taken

This illustration of the Mogul Emperor Babur consulting with his architect in the Bagh-i-Wafa near Jalalabad was one of the inspirations for the new water gardens (see pp. 66–79) and the fragrant herb garden, and helped me to crystallise my ideas.

THE COOK'S GARDEN 139

KEY

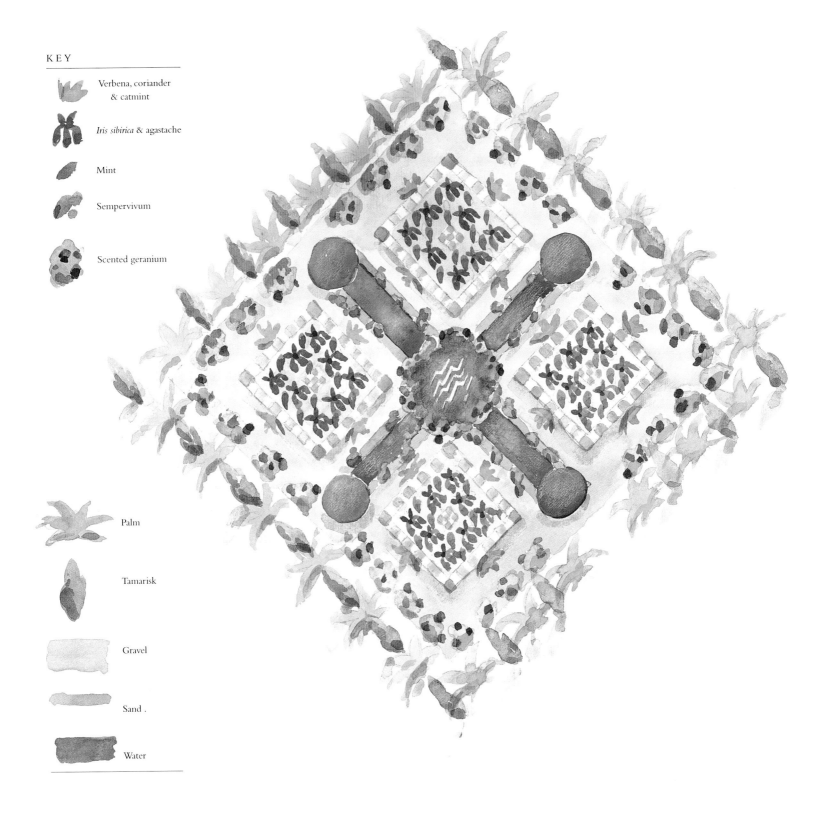

Verbena, coriander
& catmint

Iris sibirica & agastache

Mint

Sempervivum

Scented geranium

Palm

Tamarisk

Gravel

Sand .

Water

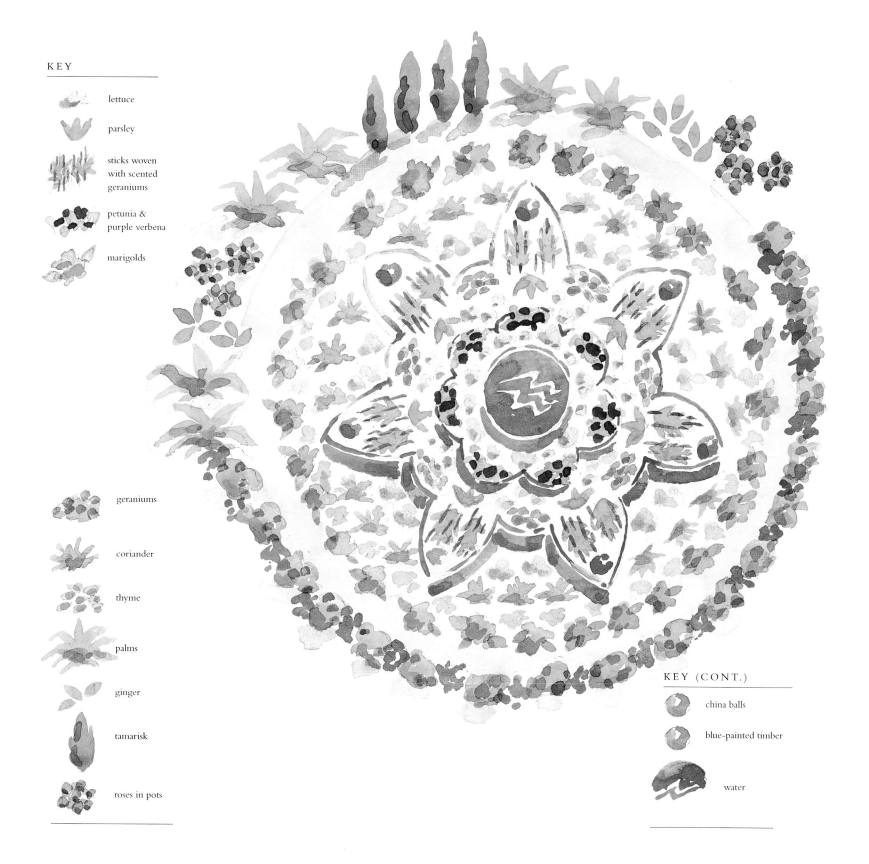

lettuce

parsley

sticks woven
with scented
geraniums

petunia &
purple verbena

marigolds

geraniums

coriander

thyme

palms

ginger

tamarisk

roses in pots

KEY (CONT.)

china balls

blue-painted timber

water

from the central motif in my study's rug. It is a circular design the shape of petals: two layers of petals made from blue-painted timber were graded by height, and a large blue water-filled bowl formed the centrepiece. It was carpeted with flowers, herbs and vegetables growing to a uniform height, its edge broken bamboo stakes to represent a rug's fringe, through which trailed bright blue lobelia and scented geraniums.

The main area of the carpet design included creeping verbenas in rose and deep blue; *Ageratum houstonianum* in tightly packed, fluffy, low-growing clumps of lavender-blue flowers; French marigolds (*Tagetes*) that never top 20cm (8in) and will grow anywhere, in orange, mahogany and yellow; pansies in deep blues; and even petunias, for they came in the ink-blue of the rug we were copying. The rounded heads of *Lobularia maritima* (syn. *Alyssum maritimum*) surrounded lettuces in fans of frilly 'Red Velvet' and red-splashed 'New Freckles', cut-leaf 'Royal Oak' and bronzed 'Rouge d'Hiver'. Parsleys with leaves flat and curled, basil leaves flavoured with lemon and cinnamon and coloured deep purple and green, and, of course, fine-leaf geraniums added their dusty fragrance.

It was bright, amusing and another suggestion for growing a regional selection of plants in a seasonal design.

The plans for these 'regional' gardens are always finalised the previous autumn, when the search for the seeds is commenced, so in March an evaluation of what seeds have been acquired and germinated can be made and the plan adjusted accordingly.

As these designs are for a planting that has a life span of five months, a dismountable structural focal point is selected: the tepee in the Native American garden, the bamboo irrigation system above the oriental vegetables, and the blue basins of water in the Islamic herb garden. It is essential to have an object to anchor the ephemeral lines of these compositions, and I plan in exactly the same way as a photographer anchors a picture by using a major structure or object as a focal point.

In a large planting just one major element may not be enough: secondary smaller stories can be introduced to break the monotony of line upon line of basically green leaves. I prefer the secondary major grouping to be plant material, such as the potted flowers and bamboo in the oriental garden, and the medicinal flowers within their canoe basket in the American garden. But too many objects and tricks can take a fun planting story into the realm of a show garden, where there are just too many ideas.

LEFT *The design for my fragrant herb garden at West Green House was cut by a cross of running water bubbling up from a central pond, flowing along canals painted the Islamic blue of Marrakesh's Majorelle gardens and terminating at wide, deep blue bowls where rose blossoms floated on cooling water. The four central gardens (1 & 2) were defined by tiles gleaned from a local salvage merchant, chosen to reflect the same blues.*

Once the Siberian iris (3) faded, blue agastache continued the height and colour into late autumn. Coriander threaded through clouds of catmint and curly-leafed pot parsley contained the square design within an aromatic border (4).

The first hole was dug in early spring and the last pictures in this sequence (5 & 6) were taken at the height of summer – four months from start to luxuriant finish.

Many of gardening's most dramatic and satisfying designs are achieved by plantings that use a single variety of flower, tree or shrub. Of course we have all shuddered at massed beds of municipal begonias, and at roadside pubs measled with huge baskets of vermilion-pink impatiens, but pause to remember the sheer thrill of a snowdrop lawn in late winter, with thousands of tiny flowers pushing through as a light dusting of snow, or the London parks, where the lawns are scattered with only jewel-coloured crocus. In Sydney in November, the purple jacaranda trees seem to

roses

I simply detested the traditional rose garden. Laid out in oblong beds surrounded by perfect bricks placed to form a jacquard pattern, it was indulged in inches-thick mulch and the impossibly healthy 'sticks' were pruned to yearly perfection. There was not a weed or any sign of life near these stems for five and a half months, so it was half a year of garden boredom.

This style of rose gardening was multiplied worldwide for it was the

A massed planting of snowdrops, Galanthus nivalis, *right across the front lawn from house to gate*

designing with a single plant

at West Green House turns the sad mid-winter grass into a carpet of white.

smother bayside suburbs in a lavender haze; in the fall the hills of New England turn blood-red when the maples blaze.

The list goes on: the fields of red poppies in France, miles of cosmos along the South African roadsides or lilac-toned lupins appearing beside lavender bushes in Sweden.

Although we do not have a countryside to plant, even in a restricted area we can achieve impact by letting favoured plants come through in rotation, or by designing predominantly with a favourite flower and enhancing it with leaves or structure. Or perhaps we design with just a small patch of trees or shrubs.

accepted way to grow roses: a single solitary species, so that it was pest-, fungus- and competition-free. If perfect roses for the flower show is what's required, then this is the way to go, but I believe that although the rose is a very special flower, its faults can be forgotten only if it is included in the overall planting design or viewed from afar.

So my roses have become accessories, for I want only bursts of their beauty rather than an over-powering bulk of colour; they reach up to be just another beautiful bloom in a border or they climb over walls or up tripods, and spill down banks so that they beguile at every angle, becoming curtains of flower that are part of the painted garden scenery.

It happens just occasionally, but when it occurs it is life-changing. At the Giardini della Landriana in central Italy I found a garden that taught more in an hour about the craft of design than a lifetime's experience has bought. Of course, in Italy, I had wandered into a garden influenced by the great English gardener the late Russell Page and made by Lavinia Taverna, its owner, working with him.

The garden at Landriana steps away from the house in garden rooms, demonstrating perfectly the gradual moving from a stylised design configuration to free-form beds with informal plantings. Then it is the revelation of a gentle hillside simply covered in just one flower.

Here on this slope the rose R. 'Mutabilis' was placed so that as the eye looked up it saw just the colour of flame buds opening to single flowers of copper pink, which faded and changed to pink, then crimson. The bushes seemed angled so as to minimise the plant's not-so-perfect superstructure. It could be called a scraggy plant but massed it was fine, airy style.

Enthralled, I planted a group of about 25 together in Australia. They liked the warmth, but although the flowers were charming the impact was minimal. So I doubled the number of bushes, planting them about 75cm (30in) apart, and swept them as a giant curve like a stream of bronzed pink. It worked, but as I have a finite area I must confess I send up through it in the mid season a huge mass of *Cosmos* 'Versailles Tetra', a deep grey pink, tall and thickly planted enough to swamp the rose and continue the impact for a few more weeks of just one plant and colour.

The hillside of *Rosa* 'Mutabilis' is a luxury planting that only a garden of this size could really indulge in, but it illustrates how simply astonishing a massed planting can be. It was also a platform for the exceptional colour of the rose, and shows how a scraggy plant can be exhibited to perfection. Its spindly shape in fact enhances the effectiveness of the display.

A more bulky rose variety would have turned the slope into just a collection of dense mounds – instead, it looks like the moving colours in Thai silk, spread out in a fragile form above the ground.

As a gardener I tend always to be searching for new design ideas, often mentally passing over great achievements from the past. After many years I revisited the Bagatelle gardens in Paris, a prodigious rose garden, where again I was awed by the roses tumbling from large free-standing columns, woven into trellis and arches, and the standard roses flowering above border rose beds. On every level, the rose surrounded, confirming my belief that roses look more compelling with light and space around them. The sunlight behind the flower was like a photographer's reflection disc, making the satin petal more luscious, outlining the pleasurable curve of its form. I could look into the rose's heart and appreciate its differing forms, and it became comprehensible why this entire garden is devoted to a single flower.

Roses, again aged and rampant, but this time in central Italy, covered the ruins of an ancient town abandoned in the Middle Ages. It had for centuries been crumbling away, forgotten, until the site was purchased by an English gardener armed with a Hillier's catalogue, who bought hundreds of roses to colonise the ruins in the lee of the overhanging mountains.

The old China rose R. 'Mutabilis' opens with petals of burnt yellow changing through pink to crimson and copper shades, so a bush is covered with simple single flowers in a mixture of these hues.

Today this casual planting of roses at Nimfa has a dream-like atmosphere, growing beside the banks of a swiftly flowing river, where water canals move so fast that they bubble and splash across the grass, bringing life and movement to the sombre grey ruins and their now masses of gigantic roses.

It again reinforced my view that roses are at their best trailing down in graceful trusses. In fact they are like supermodels – the goods just look better displayed on tall, thin limbs. The bush roses scattered very randomly through the ruins were as middle-aged ladies, their hips still not too bad, but really just a comfortable series of mid-height bumps that were pleasant but not exceptional, dotted amongst the historic remains.

Historic ruins, Parisian gardens, even aged walls, are fantasies not part of the gardening experience of most of us, but history can offer us some overlooked ideas for displaying roses.

Victorian pattern books show very solid, highly ornate timber rose stands, often embellished with fine carved finials – compelling garden statements that are beautiful objects in their own right. Climbing roses, I feel, need this theatrical support, for new roses are often prone to puberty blues, sometimes taking five years after planting to perform properly, and older roses tend to choose to favour a

certain portion on a support. These handsome stands are so much more compelling than those we tend to purchase, for they have such garden presence that the roses' vacillations can be overlooked.

When I plant a favourite climbing rose, I like to escort it all the way, accompanying it with another that flowers a little later, for I cannot bear garden structures to be used just for one flower's season. Also, I always ensure that the perennials near them are not densely planted so the new rose will not complain and sulk from being overshadowed.

The paint pot has become my new best friend. My passion for painted

supports originated in the potager, to show off trailing vegetables, but today I feel a blitz of colour behind roses in the traditional border is a timely exaggeration.

Roses attached to wires allow main branches to be lifted away for painting at pruning time, so colour can be experimented with. I like a crushed strawberry colour behind the rich pink of *Rosa* 'Constance Spry', perhaps David Austin's best rose, for it glows in front of these tones; and a thunder-storm colour, a sludgy blue-grey shade called 'Kelp', painted behind the honey-champagne *R.* 'Penny Lane' was an inspired choice, as was a warm gold that presented the flat single pink to

gold flowers of R. 'Meg' with a lavishness I'd not seen before.

A long arbour of roses once offered me one of life's true disappointments. Washed, pressed and cleaned, we children were beguiled to a garden party to see a rose arbour at peak season, but what we actually found was a gloomy tunnel with a muddy grass path beneath and the view of last year's debris above. Unhappy with the cold dark cavern below, the roses of course were on top of the tunnel, turned towards the sun. The grass as always refused to grow in darkness. I saw the same problem in the making at a very admired French garden last summer: the hazel cloister was so densely planted, there was eye-level darkness and the flowers nodded in the sky above.

Of course severe pruning would have helped allow light into the arbour, but if I were to cover a path with rambling roses, I'd now place a series of free-standing arches along it, resisting the temptation to join them and allowing at least 1.5m (5ft) between. This allows the sun to surround the rose completely, coaxing it to scatter its flowers and encouraging grass and border planting beneath. And at high season the rose's growth stretches neatly to the next arch, giving the same effect as an arbour.

The choice of a not too rampant rambling rose – such as *Rosa*

LEFT *Designer Kathryn Gustafson's arbour, using blooms of a dominant colour, is a striking way of displaying roses in a contemporary style.*

RIGHT *For me, David Austin's most beautiful rose is the sugar-pink* R. *'Constance Spry'.*

'Sombreuil', a beloved creamy white tea rose – to cover a wide arch can help alleviate this problem – or try the delicately tinted R. 'Alida Lovett', a double shell-pink rose that grows to 3.5m (12ft) – and permit more manageable pruning of rampant rambling roses. A medium-sized pillar rose nearly reaches to an average arch's centre, leaving a gap that will allow warmth and light to penetrate. Good plant catalogues list to what height roses will grow: it is important to choose the right-sized plant when designing with roses.

Graceful colonnades are perhaps the most difficult garden feature to achieve. Don't be afraid of tall columns, for squat columns – or even average-sized poles – will look even dumpier once the crossbeams arrive and their length is covered by roses or other vines. I find the eye follows the flowering branches down, optically foreshortening the arbour's height.

I feel that a colonnade close to a house should look as if it is joined to the building at ground-floor ceiling height, or at eaves level on a one-storey building. Wrongly proportioned, colonnades can give a façade the look of Frida Kahlo, whose dark eyebrows across the face are never forgotten, creating a too strong and deep line where it is not expected.

Roses are more likely to flower from their base if the canes are wrapped around a column: if led up a long vertical wire, the flowers and leaves are being trained away from their support.

The current trends in garden design are leading us towards sculptural plants, hard finishes, dispensing with the warm and fuzzy details. But I cannot live without a rose, especially a climbing or rambling rose, for just one truss tumbling in the right spot can be like that last long feather on a hat, a nonchalant sweep that lifts a perfectly acceptable design to another level, a throwaway gesture that means nothing and everything.

fragrant rose gardens

I am of the belief that all fragrant rose gardens should be stepped down as a 'sunken' garden with a terraced retaining wall, or enclosed by a hedge or fence.

Medieval manuscripts illustrate enclosed rose gardens surrounded by trellis as walls or forming tunnels that shelter the roses, containing any zephyr of scent and providing the climbing varieties with a very decorative home.

But climbing roses are strong plants and will in time crush their supports, so they must be of an enduring material, poles of cement, iron or perhaps the hardest wood available. Adequate footings are important, for it's an impossible chore to re-erect them when flowers and leaves are there.

At pathside, bush roses provide delight. I adore the Bourbon roses, whose opulent flowers of silky texture are teacup shapes above substantial well-rounded bushes. Their stunning beauty in late spring and autumn, their fragrance and quartered blooms all add up to the storybook rose.

The embodiment of the perfect rose: left to right, R. *'Königen von Dänemark',* R. *'Fantin-Latour' and* R. *'La Reine Victoria'.*

Wherever I go, I plant:

✄ **'Bourbon Queen'**: rose pink, deeply cupped double blooms. Heady sweet perfume. Amazing in spring with lush growth. 1.4m (4½ft).

✄ **'Honorine de Brabant'**: a rose striped in shades of purple pink. Vigorous and healthy. 1.5m (5ft).

✄ **'Souvenir de St Anne's'**: looks to be nearly single with long golden stamens above cream pink petals.

✄ **'Souvenir de la Malmaison'**: this is my dream rose. Cupped, quartered, the colour of face powder, but it hates rain, wind and humidity and is coated with powdery mildew before spring is over. One season in three it performs well, bringing me to my knees in despair, but I still grow it as it's irresistible. Also in this category are 'Mme Isaac Pereire', 'Louise Odier', 'Mme Pierre Oger' and 'La Reine Victoria'. If they love you, they are supreme must-haves.

✄ **'Variegata di Bologna'** 1909: one of the best striped roses to add some oomph to overly pretty pink rose beds. Some say it looks like black-currants swirled through cream. It's very double and very fragrant.

Recently I saw *Anemanthele lessoniana* filming through the solid rounded cups of 'Reine des Violettes' and the old gallica R. 'Camaieux', wonderfully splashed with crimson on white that fades to lilac grey. The gentler grass broke the solid splash of rose peta;, giving the bed an ethereal quality I'd not seen achieved with roses before.

I also try to hide my bushes of pink roses in strong swathes of rich colour. The wiry 1.2m (4ft) stems of *Astrantia major* 'Hadspen's Blood' make a thicket of ruby-red pincushions that debunks the Sugar Plum Fairy look that masses of these roses can make.

Others in the 'must-have' heritage category are:

✄ **'Blanchefleur'**: a centifolia rose that is a pompon of milky white petals, quartered from a central green eye. It has a rich fragrance, but again it flowers so profusely in spring that the bush seems lost under the abundance of flower.

✄ **'Devoniensis'**: a large creamy white rose that deserves a place in all gardens. Fragrance of lemon tea.

✄ **'Fantin-Latour'**: this centifolia is the perfect sugar-pink rose on a superb bush. Delicious fragrance from huge cupped flowers that open to wide flattish blooms.

✄ **'Königin von Dänemark'**: an alba rose, very double, very fragrant, with pink blooms so heavy the branches droop under the weight.

✄ **'Roseraie de l'Haÿ'**: a turn-of-the-century rose, open and crimson with a scent of honey and cloves.

FROM DAVID AUSTIN:

- **'Charles Rennie Mackintosh'**: large cupped deep lilac-pink blooms that are deeply fragrant.
- **'Constance Spry'**: absolutely the most beautiful of Austin roses, with large bowls of sugar-pink flowers. The fragrance is the scent of myrrh and the plant is so vigorous it climbs a pillar happily.

Folk tales persist that only 'old' roses have fragrance, but David Austin roses have some of the most fragrant flowers, and many hybrid tea varieties have the richest aromas. Fragrance in a rose depends on its original parent, it's not the fault of modern rose breeders.

Struggling with a recalcitrant rose recently, I felt that a rose reflects the journey of our lives. Both are welcomed with joy and carefully nurtured. In youth there is intensive training and gradually a flowering begins. In mid-life confidence comes and a fine display greets all. But in maturity the supports are broken and the rose tosses its head and does its own thing, climbing over walls into trees, totally uncaring of what others think as it becomes the most wondrous plant. But then the wildness reaches its zenith and gradually the over-extended plant is cut back and finally disposed of.

Sounds familiar?

tulips

Like the dancers at the Moulin Rouge, tulips with sculptured lily shapes, icicle fringes and plumes are dazzling, sassy and slightly bizarre as they dance in the crisp spring air of my garden at West Green.

Other flowers and leaves approach spring at a pianissimo level, a soft scattering of shy petals and unfurling tendrils, but tulips open in a triumphant crescendo, absolutely self-confident in their splendour, shining stems in need of a perfect setting.

Traditionally, tulips are used as massed banks of colour, planted to achieve bulk optical shock, but I like to treat them as courtesans to be escorted by the plant world's mature roués, the latters' maturity a foil to the flowers' wilful exuberance.

Emotionally, tulips are equated with exotica and the dissipation of seventeenth-century Dutch fortunes. But in early spring my most wonderful garden colours and shapes are to be found in the gothic remains of the potager's old vegetables. Am I creating a misalliance by placing tulips among

Sassy and dazzling, tulips can simply light up gardens for four months from early spring if you select varieties that will flower in succession.

them? I don't think so, for who has ever turned down a striking escort? The outcome can be exciting. So in early spring the tulip, the now dominant flower in my garden, is supported by the leaves and forms of vegetables.

I have always thought the stems of Brussels sprouts, knobbled with vegetable bunions and crowned by curving leaves, have an aristocratic air. So 'Falstaff', a burgundy Brussels sprout variety, has become a companion to *Tulipa* 'Blue Parrot', its petticoats billowing from a deep plum centre, and together they create a vertical pattern in the spring potager. Spikes of *Fritillaria persica* punctuate these regal tones with nodding bells turned down like monks' cowls.

Try echoing the roundness of the large, winter-maturing Savoy cabbage 'January King', or the purplish 'Red Flame' cabbage, with the mahogany red of *Tulipa* 'Bird of Paradise', an extraordinary parrot style, beside it. Then perhaps consider the black sheen

The peony-style tulip T. 'Allegretto' is like a solo act, dominating the other flowers in an early-spring potager.

of rhubarb chard leaves, whose luminous ruby-red stems make a demonic foil for *T.* 'Black Parrot'.

A palette of sherbet orange, browns and golds is achieved by weaving the stalks of gold and yellow 'Bright Lights' chard through 60cm (2ft) stands of *Fritillaria imperialis* 'Aurora', with its towers of orange bells crowned by slim green leaves, and then follow with multi-petalled cups of peony-shaped *Tulipa* 'Orange Princess'. For true glamour, dash a handful of blackberry-coloured mid-season *Tulipa* 'Paul Scherer' through the old nasturtium shades of *T.* 'Orange Princess', together with rusty-toned wallflowers.

But it is the architectural giant kales that make the most handsome companions for tulips. Curtains of burgundy kale 'Redbor', 1.2m (4ft) high, create an intense glow for tulips in lavender pinks, while the deepest blue-green permed leaves of kale 'Tuscan Black' anchor the fragile quality of lemon *Tulipa* 'West Point', a lily-style tulip, swaying above annually sown forget-me-nots.

To achieve these effects in spring, the winter-maturing vegetables are planted the previous summer, ensuring fresh winter fare and next springtime's style. Often two rows of a plant are sown, with one row harvested in winter, then replaced by tulips to complement the vegetables' colour and shape. So where in late summer ferny, dwarf white cosmos tickled the new green and white leeks, in spring, erect single white *Tulipa* 'Maureen' takes its place, matching the mature leek's height above a scattering of winter violas. Or, as a fresh line of multicoloured chard echoes the fiesta colours of *Eschscholzia californica* (Californian poppy) in summer, the colour scheme is repeated five months later with a collection of viridiflora tulips creating a similar rainbow against the vivid vegetable stalks.

I sow seeds of 'Bright Lights' Swiss chard in trays, picking out the colour seedlings I require for a particular pattern. However, seeds are available in individual colours, including scarlet 'Rhubarb Chard', the white-stemmed 'Lucullus' and 'Bright Yellow', with its gold stalks.

Early spring pots are filled with vegetables and tulips. *T.* 'Texas Gold', with stems that twist like some deep-sea creature, curves through last season's sprouts and fresh green chard.

Layered bulbs will extend the pots' flowering. Consider planting the late-spring lemon-scented *Tulipa* 'Bellona', for this parrot tulip will unfurl to enjoy the later warmth of the brimming pot.

With Lilliputian species leading the way, tulips can blaze across the garden at West Green House from February, commencing a tulip season that, with careful selection, can last five months.

T. humilis 'Violet Green' flowers first, then a shriek of scarlet arrives with 'Wilsoniana', *T. praestans* 'Fusilier' and *T. greigii* 'Red Riding Hood', which carries these red mini-skirts through to April.

I am naturalising these miniature tulips and left undisturbed they are beginning to multiply under the deciduous trees. Planted beside an area where the grass is mowed to form later paths, they are quickly removed after flowering, for the nurserymen tell me they can leave disease.

Many have beautifully marked leaves. *T. praestans* 'Unicum', for example, is an offspring of 'Fusilier' but with butter-edged leaves, while the dark-striped leaves of lemon-yellow *T. greigii* 'Plaisir' could be grown for their smartness alone. *T. kaufmanniana* 'Gluck' hybrids are triangular candy stripes of yellow and red above speckled striped leaves, and *T. tarda*'s leaves and flowers resemble ground-hugging gold stars.

daffodils and bluebells

It is twelve years since I planted a birch wood of over 500 trees at Kennerton Green to honour my mother's last wishes, and I have now had time to reflect on what is, probably, my most extravagant gardening episode. I acknowledge it was definitely not the correct planting for the climate, but it has given great pleasure and now provides a rolling woodland floor for a wild garden.

In the last days of winter the white trunks of the birch trees are a stark forest of shiny white fingers, generally backed by the bright blue skies of the season, and it is time to admire the impact of just one species multiplied, as nature sets up a rolling timetable of a new bulb every few weeks for the next three months.

As a suggestion of leaf greens the twigs, the woodland floor breaks into rich golden yellow as a dwarf *Narcissus bulbocodium* var. *conspicuus*, the hoop-petticoat daffodil, enacts Wordsworth's poem in miniature. This miniature daffodil has multiplied a hundredfold here, but in England it is not so happy for me where I have tried to introduce it. Instead, the diminutive trumpets of *Narcissus* 'Tête-à-tête' have naturalised well under very dense shade. An entire garden of open-faced daffodils gives brash, blithesome colour. They are carefree plants that flower, fade and need not leave unwanted leaves if smaller varieties are chosen.

Carefully selected daffodils can bloom in continuing swathes from mid winter to mid spring – four months. I've chosen predominantly white narcissus for the English lake field, concluding with the flat faces of Pheasant's Eye as the roses start to bud.

As I comment on the passing of this early daffodil carpet, the main event – the untold numbers of bluebells and scillas planted by hand, consuming vast patches of grass – encompasses the woodland planting. Their height and wider leaf swamp the finishing daffodil.

My cup runneth over, for this is the garden Mother wanted – and then I

Spring's final daffodil – the white-petalled, dark orange-cupped 'Pheasant's Eye', flowering in the lakeside field at West Green House.

can't bear to go into it any more as I watch garden visitors wheel prams across, small boys with sticks beat the bluebells to death, and photographers with enough equipment for a *Vogue* shoot assure me they haven't mulched one down.

Cross as I am, I truly cannot blame them, for again the impression of a field of just one plant is prodigious. It entices the feet away from mown paths into a haze of blue infinity. In a suburban garden a friend has created the same effect under a group of deciduous trees with a dense planting of muscari: the saturated blue colour encourages the eye to think the patch of blue is larger than it is.

As the grass quietly swamped the spent bluebells, I always wished that there was just one plant that would grow tall enough to skim this green field for a further month until the grass loses its gloss and is cut down!

irises

The blue English irises planted under the gold laburnum arch in another part of the garden at Kennerton Green had never prospered, so the year before I had them dug up and potted. After much walking back and forth I decided they were the right height to swim above the meadow grass, an important enough flower to add definite colour and shape above long green strands. Now their sapphire-blue flowers are a final conspicuous statement under the lacy leaves of the birch, ready to end their season as mowing commences.

But this type of planting needs the definition of a mower path or a block of strong colour shot through it to give cohesion. Blue iris in many forms now fulfil this role. The focal point the glade – a waterlily-filled pond – encircles hosts huge banks of blue and white *Iris ensata*, and now a new river of *I. sibirica* 'Papillon' snakes beneath the trees.

Iris sibirica is one of the most elegant plants, with tall, grass-like leaves and soft flowers on long stems. Planted in large groups it becomes pure design, its leaves still graceful even when the flower concludes.

Sky blue is again captured in the *Iris germanica* that breaks the edges of the encircling road. *I.* 'Jane Phillips' is a faithful friend, one of the most tolerant of this style of iris.

From the earliest days of spring till the first of summer, just one type of flower at a time covers this woodland floor. It is, I believe, simple, understated and a satisfying style of gardening – a naturalised garden, controlled.

In Sweden I once saw martagon lilies planted in drifts, in an old apple orchard above the white foam of cow parsley. Their musky pink Turk's caps enchanted on dark stems. I tried to replicate the sensation in Hampshire, but in this temperature zone they do not flower in concert, so when planning a rolling planting it is important to choose varieties appropriate to your climate zone in order to achieve the most striking displays.

LEFT *By snaking a single line of Louisiana iris through a wide canal of water, designer Bunny Guinness carries the eye through her garden.*

FAR LEFT *Beside the canal a grouping of dark* Iris sibirica *echoes the colour of the water iris and the intensity of the colour is relieved with the paler flowers of* Iris laevigata.

steel

The influences for design by colour surround us everywhere in the garden, not just obvious colour but more thoughtful hues too: the abstract colourless space between droplets of moving water, the suggestion of repeated colour in a distant line of sparrows along a telegraph wire, or the suggestion of colour through dappled shade.

It was this abstract shading I was aware of on a warm afternoon

for it was as unwelcoming to humans as a grey prison wall. While in Australia, a wide bed of excellent natives, all in the grey shades of our environment, were a wonderful collection of cut, serrated and spiked leaf shapes drowsing under a hot sun. Politically correct and heat-resistant, they were at that season utterly dreary, which was a shame, for it was high summer and time to relish more drama in the garden.

The first 'grey' garden to enthuse me had been the late Madame de

designing with colour

standing in the shade of an old grey gum tree when I mused why it is that there is no answering spark in my soul for very acceptable borders of grey plants.

I had seen three styles of grey border that season. One, in England, where mounds of small grey-green leaves in groups of varying heights looked just depressing under skies of low grey light. In the western USA, a brilliant designer had created a barrier of sharp abstract shapes in bold grey yuccas, agaves and cactus, in a garden that was so lethally sharp, it was better to look at it from the safety of the car,

Vesian's garden in southern France. Here she had taken mainly the regional plants of the garrigue and by precise clipping had created a vista of rounded, textural shapes, enlivened by the exclamation marks of vertical cypresses, a sculpture garden of living grey masonry. At the Giardini della Landriana in central Italy, an alley of silver-white plants (the design suggested many years ago by Russell Page) sparkled despite the dusty white sky above.

Both these Mediterranean gardens were brilliant interpretations of silver-grey gardening. But they both used

plants that could be described as gardening 'toughies', many of which despised the wet of most cool temperate gardens and lacked any element of softness.

I was at this stage actively looking at 'grey plants' for my blue border, which, I felt, was becoming just too charming. It needed sophisticated colour, a dash of style, cut and design. Somehow, I had to find plants that were statuesque but not belligerent curiosities, a textural mixture that was both velvet and dungarees, and good garden architecture, not just the charms of Colefax and Fowler!

A silvery grass, *Miscanthus sinensis* 'Morning Light', arched with fine strong leaves, gave systematic structure

Plants in every shade of steel – a mixture of blues, grey and silvery white – fill the new gallery border at Kennerton Green. Mostly Mediterranean-climate plants, here Euphorbia characias wulfenii, Echium candicans *and* Artemisia *'Valerie Fiennes', are lit by small clumps of bright blue irises.*

to groups of *Delphinium* 'Gillian Dallas' that are a soft, atmospheric, dusty blue-grey. These formed the backbone of the planting in England.

Echiums adore my garden in Australia, but in Hampshire they come from the greenhouse at frost's end, a sub-story to the delphiniums, but well worth trying to coax into flower by summer's last days. I grow *Echium candicans*, whose giant grey candle is studded with tiny dark blue flowers, and *Echium pininana*, with silver lanceolate leaves that hide flowers of lavender rose, together with other varieties when I can locate the seeds.

Echiums flower in their second year and in warm climates generally live to their third year. In Australia another plant is always placed beneath the current flower to ensure the border's continuing shape.

Between my garden giants, like a wave of shimmering silken fabric, the common larkspur *Consolida ajacis* 'Earl Grey', in drop-dead gorgeous shades of battleship grey, is sown *in situ*, providing movement that suggests a brooding sea. This is a flower bulk that pulls soaring plants together, a shapeless mass to anchor stronger forms. Another soft grouping, as mysterious beneath their hoods as a grey monastic order, is *Aconitum* 'Stainless Steel', with hints of lilac tones. It is a tough reliable border plant

70cm (30in) tall. It is planted behind silver-grey *Eryngium maritimum* and *E. giganteum* 'Silver Ghost', a heavily frosted and more advanced form of *E. giganteum* 'Miss Willmott's Ghost'. To balance this collection of spiky stars, I have placed the low-growing *E. alpinum* 'Superbum' in front, and tucked around ground-hugging *Euphorbia myrsinites*, to form a sulphur-blue mat in front.

Iris germanica, the tough bearded iris, dislikes my cold English soil, and weeks of wet mean a troubled existence for a pewter-grey iris, 'Pewter Treasure', so its tall shape will be echoed by the grey-white felted leaves of *Verbascum bombyciferum* 'Arctic Summer', a velvet-soft javelin that gives a fluorescent-light effect to neighbouring plants.

The centre leaves of *Artemisia ludoviciana* 'Valerie Finnis' also suggest grey fur, which darkens as the plant reaches its comforting rounded shape, a tough but velvety plant form that bears repeating in a border pattern.

Into these grey whites I like to place *Echinops sphaerocephalus* 'Arctic Glow', frosted balls of near white on red stems with silver-grey leaves, and, if water and dappled shade allow, mounds of grey *Hosta sieboldiana* var. *elegans* which has a surface sheen. Most grey plants have hairy leaves, so it provides a polished contrast – but only

if the slug and snail population is under control.

I am convinced that these pests take the same length of time to eat a hosta leaf as Grandmother's grey Persian cat could be persuaded to adorn the bed for a photograph – not long! But last year the hostas survived the summer nearly intact and I was told that the arrival of toads had achieved what insecticides could not.

Flowers and leaves that shine and reflect light create important sparkle and make more sombre plant combinations live. Charles Quest-Ritson, the super rose specialist, has guided me to a grey rose called *Rosa* 'Gray Pearl'. For me, a satin rose petal, with its form of tactile richness, will gather together the plants of severe shape and humanise many of the prima donnas of the garden world, welding together at mid height an exotic collection in, predominantly, the colour of steel.

LEFT Hosta sieboldiana elegans *is a polished contrast to the hairy leaves of most grey plants.*

CENTRE & RIGHT Globe artichoke (Cynara scolymus) *and the closely related cardoon* (Cynara cardunculus) *are among my favourite 'steel' plants, with the added bonus of striking architectural form.*

earth and oil

The names are exotic: terracotta, umber and sienna, warming Italian imagery; or luscious: as coffee, butterscotch and chocolate; or comforting: thoughts of russet, copper or conkers. Tones of the earth, soft harmonies of stronger hues.

Then there are the colours that lurk further into the earth's crust, mysterious underworld colours of dark oil, inky purples and sludgy browns. All are unusual colours that add depth to colour design.

Too many gelato-coloured flowers tend to make a garden, like the ice-cream, sweet and inconsequential, like another meringue wedding dress, all froth and no style.

Browns are classic colours that I like to arrange together, especially the shades of caramel, placed to grow in a pyramid design like a *croquembouche* – the perfect design shape – a triangle, where the flowers look like the toffee cascading all over from top to bottom.

Plant breeders are providing wondrous new plants to indulge these fantasies. Nothing gives more dominant height than the new hollyhock *Althaea* 'Chestnut Brown', mixed with a beige-shaded *A.* 'Chamois', to form the axis of a summer's garden. I've mixed these colours with the coral brown of *Macleaya* 'Kelways Coral Plume', whose fine plumes rise above oak-cut blue-grey leaves, a perennial that rises to 1.8m (6ft) by August.

The copper flowers of *Verbascum* 'Cotswold Beauty' are treated as an annual as they will not overwinter for me, and the new *V.* 'Copper Rose', with spikes of flat flowers in buff, tan and every shade in between, flowers throughout the summer but does not set seed. The new seeds I buy are pollinated by hand. I despair of these plants, but they are unique tones capturing every shade in this range and echoing at least one hue of every plant I place here. However, I have now been introduced to a new range of perennial verbascums by nursery-woman Marina Christopher. She says that *V.* 'Norfolk Dawn' is all the shades of a McVities biscuit, *V.* 'Patricia' more bronze and *V.* 'Hiawatha' a mixture of bronze and purple. I wait anxiously to see if they are as stunning in year two!

Providing an exquisite joy are the thousands of tiny Jersey fudge bells of *Digitalis ferruginea,* now joined by *D.* parviflora, foxglove bells of the deepest chocolate, packed along 60cm (2ft) stalks like baby cobra heads with lemon fangs. Their place is taken over in July by *Hemerocallis* 'Ed Murray', a 'bottom of the claret bottle' sludge, and the bitter chocolate leaves of *Heucherella* 'Quicksilver'.

Another high-summer curiosity is the annual *Calendula* 'Coffee Cream', with splattered quill-like brown petals, and *Nasturtium* 'Black Velvet', an oily brown ground cover that is not at all rampant.

A tree with a trunk that looks like the family's best piece of mahogany furniture is *Prunus serrula* 'Miyako', a small flat-topped flowering cherry, suitable for smaller gardens, and offering dappled shade for the dusky hellebore *Helleborus purpurascens*, whose murky colour ushers in any grouping of brown-toned plants in early spring.

If space allows, I like to plant in groups, so that the story – be it in leaf, flower or shape – is reinforced. At West Green House, a group of five of these prunus trees has been planted with the hellebores in a teardrop-shape bed, mixed with fritillarias. The dark chocolaty shades in *Fritillaria davisii, F. camschatcensis* and *F. michailovskyi* have been scattered with *F. meleagris,* the snake's-head fritillary, but they are proving to be tiny nuggets of edible truffles for a population of squirrels and rabbits that not even the ferrets can dissuade.

The warm tones of a sunburnt country are here in the pinky-brown spikes of Echium *'Pride of Madeira', grown in an Australian country garden.*

The colours I am now talking about have turned from the brogue browns to the brown-black range of plants which has expanded enormously. Flying across the Rocky Mountains recently I looked down on to some of the world's most inspiring scenery. Snow still dusted the high peaks, but the great weathered canyons were fired earth, cut by deep gorges of purple-black scars, highlighting the sheer drama of the scene. I think this illustrates the most effective way these moody-hued plants can both act as highlights to a neighbour's richer colour and at the same time draw attention to themselves.

Flowers and leaves in brilliant purple and purple browns make the plants in ochre, umber and sienna look very smart, by weaving a suggestion of shadows through them. These old earth colours of an ageing sun generally grow into generous confident banks that can take the borders over now as the gardener relaxes at season's end.

Try large blocks of *Achillea* 'Terracotta', with its tiny flowers grouped as on a flat plate, or the round shape and smart mix of colours – burnt orange, crimson and apricot – of *Dahlia* 'Diablo'. Both look just more glowing beside *Salvia verticillata* 'Purple Rain' or enclosed by *Euphorbia amygdaloides* 'Purpurea', its leaf absolute structure from darkest purple to purple brown lit by flowers in lime yellow.

Consider grouping *Lysimachia ciliata* 'Firecracker', which has small bright yellow flowers atop its 90cm (3ft) mahogany-purple stems and leaves, and the earth-toned *Helenium* 'Moerheim Beauty', solid blocks like desert buttes that are of the same height, with a bank of the richest purple flowers of *Lobelia* x *gerardii* 'Vedrariensis' or the gauzy branches of sea lavender, *Limonium platyphyllum*, as a haze of violet nearby.

I like to place the brooding colours together, one drift enclosing another, interspersing them with spikes of jewelled tones. The indigo delphinium 'Faust' looks vivid supported by *Salvia* x *sylvestris* 'Blaugher', as bright as Las Vegas purple neon, with a wide band of the smoky purple leaves of *Sedum* 'Ruby Glow' at its feet. Or try a Mars Bar combination of a dusty pink foxglove,

Digitalis x *mertonensis*, rising above the milk-chocolate leaves of the simple pink-flowered *Geranium* 'Pink Spice' with the fudge and white *Iris* 'Light Laughter'.

As night's pall descends, the modern garden can be transformed by a galaxy of lighting wizardry, and dark shapes in the garden: tall trunks, weeping trees and fronds re-emerge as floodlit black silhouettes, perhaps more important now than when surrounded by daytime colour. Backlit topiary in courtyards can be treated as stage scenery: portable dark colour in pots to be positioned for the most admiration. I am addicted to my collection, reminiscent of eighteenth-century garden-theatre shapes, and it continues to grow.

A double avenue of pruned winter trees on London's South Bank outlined in dark lights of iridescent blue made stark and arresting sculpture; their impact made me stop and think about colour in a dark garden. Light captured in the sombre tones of a Japanese lacquer pot, the deep silver fire within steel on gun-metal grey, or the tarnished glow in bronze, reflect new ideas for dark colour.

Old theatre curtains remind us that deep rich reds capture and hold light, so a mixture of these hues could be the chosen design colour for a candlelit patio. The imagery of a night garden calls for fragrance: a romantic treatment of a rich rose sweet pea *Lathyrus odoratus* 'Zorya Rose' intertwined with the nearly black *L. o.* 'Midnight', growing from highly glossed pots and rising behind the polished black leaves of *Ophiopogon planiscapus* 'Nigrescens' to soften the patio edge and reflect every prism, would fulfil exemplary night-colour requirements.

Black glass has the reflection of midnight oil when holding black capsicums and deep purple aubergines on a hot Sydney night. It is all pure theatre, but adventurous choices in plants, textures and colours can bring different enchantments into our garden concepts.

There are more flowers and leaves of deep and moody colour to be used in gardens designed around the shades of earth and oil.

✻ **Alcea rosea** 'Nigra': maroon-black satin hollyhock. It loathes humidity. Touches 1.5m (5ft) tall. Full sun, mid summer.

✻ **Aquilegia viridiflora**: totally chocolate-brown caps with long spurs. Grows 30cm (12in) tall. Spring. *A. vulgaris* 'Magpie' or 'William Guinness' produces bonnets of black and white petals in early spring that will self-seed throughout the border. Grows 60cm (24in) tall.

✻ **Centaurea cyanus** (cornflower): a black ball of annual flower. Grows 35cm (15in) tall. Full sun, summer.

✻ **Dianthus barbatus** 'Sooty': fragrant deepest maroon-black satin flowers from May to late spring. Grows 35cm (15in) tall. Full sun, spring border. *D.* 'Velvet Lace' has fragrant black double flowers, trimmed in white. Grows 30cm (12in) tall. Full sun, summer.

✻ **Haloragis erecta** 'Melton Bronze': a serrated bronze-black leaf for the border's edge. Smart all season and grows 30cm (12in) tall. Full sun.

✻ **Heuchera** 'Chocolate Ruffles': darkest brown leaves forming good clumps. Grows 60cm (24in) tall. Dappled light, from early spring.

✻ **Ipomoea** 'Carmen': a strong black-red vine of exceptional vigour. Full sun, summer.

✻ **Iris chrysographes** 'Black Forest': midnight-black iris. Needs a drained gravelly position. Grows 45cm (18in) tall. Full sun, mid spring.

✻ **Lysimachia atropurpurea**: it looks like a wine-black lavender, but will tolerate dappled shade. Flowers from mid spring and grows 45cm (18in) tall.

✻ **Nemophila** 'Penny Black': a ground cover in spring, frilled in white. Grows 30cm (12in) tall. Dappled light.

✻ **Papaver somniferum** 'Black Peony': a black-red fully double self-seeding poppy. Absolute showstopper. Grows 90cm (3ft) tall. Full sun, late spring.

✻ **Salpiglossis** 'Chocolate Box': black-red trumpets for summer's end. Grows 45cm (18in) tall. Full sun.

✻ **Scabiosa atropurpurea** 'Ace of Spades': fragrant pincushion flowers as dark as can be. Grows 90cm (3ft) tall. Full sun, mid-summer border.

✻ **Viola nigra**: the black pansy for pot and border edge. Grows 22.5cm (9in) tall. Full sun, from spring.

Plants of the darkest tones act as compelling full stops, punctuating a planting. Here Hemerocallis 'Ed Murray' (left) and Echeveria 'Black Knight' are garden inkspots.

citrus

These are strident colours considered by many to be at the bottom of the good-taste heap, an image that unfortunately is reinforced by processed food, where the word 'citrus' is often interpreted as violent colour and acid flavour, and by the vile fashion shades that are always the remnants in the end-of-season sales.

But citrus can evoke some most beautiful imagery: the warm sharp smell of oranges in piles in a North African souk, the espaliered lemon on a stone wall near Sorrento, or the heady fragrance of its small star-shaped flower in a wedding bouquet. In a garden design citrus can be interpreted as either sharp and iridescent or mellow, as in a jar of marmalade where strands of dark peel meld with tone upon tone of rich orange.

I think it was those dark caramelised strands that first induced me to put lines of deep colour into a new border that was for flowers of this colour alone. Now, a long curve of mahogany-leafed *Astroplex* var. 'Rubrea', sown as the first plantings were placed, self-seeds annually, making a 120cm (4ft) wall of strong colour which both acts as a foil to this strident colour and prevents it from intruding too much across the path to flower groups of other tones nearby.

It also became a framework to build colour groupings from. Its structure was an anchor for this 20m (65ft) of citrus, and prevented it from becoming just a herbaceous border of strong, saturating colour.

Bronze-green *Magnolia grandiflora* were placed along the entire length, cut in 1.8m (6ft) pyramids. They were matched by tripods with plants that have a more spatial quality: *Clematis* 'Bill MacKenzie', a rampant airy vine with nodding yellow bonnets and fine seed heads that recall the long tapering hands of a ghostly form, cohabiting with the English rose *R.* 'Teasing Georgia, a burnished yellow, its petal cups redolent with good fragrance.

When one comes to design the planting of a herbaceous border using these colours, the majority of blooms seem to be daisy-shaped. Under many different names these simple flowers are friendly and easy to grow – in fact my gratitude to them knows no bounds, for when I first started gardening in the harsh climate of southern New South Wales it was these hardy faces, mostly of South African or American prairie origin, that would survive.

Eremurus 'Cleopatra' rises in tall, glowing spears of burnt orange up to 120cm (4ft) high and provides arresting structure during its flowering season.

Most like my English garden too, but some must be planted only once the frosts have departed. Banks of buff, cream and shades of orange *Osteospermum sinuate* 'Pastel Silks' – an annual in the UK, perennial in warmer climates – meld together other warm mellow shades, while the colour contrasts in *Calendula* 'Greenheart', with orange petals and a green eye, and *Coreopsis verticillata* 'Moonbeam', with a green eye and lemon petals, are sharp tones. Look through the catalogues for these daisy forms under the names *Gaillardia, Rudbeckia, Artemisia, Tagetes, Helianthus* and *Mesembryanthemum*, to name a few. These plants will form into dense clumps, loving the long hot days of summer.

Huge clumps of these mellow flowers can be like custard, delicious but boring. I like to break them with fine tall plants: the awkward arms of *Cephalaria gigantea* with a light lemon pincushion flower perched absurdly atop, and the pure architecture of euphorbias, especially *Euphorbia characias wulfenii*, 120cm (4ft) of fine leaves and lime flowers. Tall lilies, the apricot *Lilium* 'African Queen', preceded by rich yellow *L.* 'Golden Splendour', are citrus for early autumn. They need support, so I place them beneath earlier-flowering roses of the same hues. The amber *Rosa* 'Raymond Carver', a modern shrub

rose with flowers of old-fashioned shape, is very large and its green foliage makes a strong cage. And so a dull spot comes back to life!

Leaf must break this over-abundance of flower. Chosen just for its leaf, the slow-growing *Acer palmatum* 'Orange Dream' lit by deeply cut orange leaves over layers of gold and lime – a sunrise beside boisterous *Sambucus racemosa* 'Sutherland Gold', a handsome bush of fine feathery gold foliage. Then, at pathside, the buff to rust foliage of *Heuchera* 'Amber Waves'

with *Helichrysum* 'Sulphur Light', its flowers like yellow knobs on fine mounds of grey, both insisting on a dry place.

I think these tones look excellent when placed together, melding tone upon tone, but where they will also act as arc light to flowers in purples and blues, or become lit fires behind clear reds, they are invaluable. But I do find variegated green and gold, especially in evergreen leaves, difficult and awkward to place. This is equally true from 'Swane's Gold' in a *Cupressus* to

varieties of pittosporums and even to vividly striped hostas.

The majority of the flowers in this colour range are sun-worshippers, so, in grouping these bronzes, golds and coppers, why not place an object that catches the sun's rays – such as a polished brass pot or a sundial in shining tones, or a line of golden poles?

As summer fades I introduce baskets painted hot marigold, yellow and old gold and filled with yellow calla lilies to the West Green House borders.

LEFT & RIGHT *All the shades of a jar of marmalade are melded together in the sunshine tones of a collection of* Achillea. *Included in these borders are* A. *'Forncett Fletton',* A. *'Moonshine',* A. *'Terracotta' and* A. *'Walther Funcke'.*

Of course these colours are symbols of the goodness of the sun, and sun-ripened vegetables make the most emotive vegetable garden patterns. A simple grid of orange pumpkins laid out each year on the garden's cleared ground are like giant setting suns – full stops declaring that the growing year is over – and gourds can be stacked in small pyramids or placed to edge paths. Used this way these tough-shelled vegetables can give another month of pattern to a bare garden.

There is a childlike simplicity in these tones. Sunny and infectious, I equate them with rustic rather than classic or sophisticated design, a style of fun colour emphasis. So when using these tones in a garden design I tend to consign them to areas of abundance: packed herbaceous borders, the bountiful vegetable garden and children's play areas; but then I stop and remember the orangery at Versailles, where in summer the courtyard in front becomes a grid of white boxes each containing an orange

tree. Similarly, in southern Spain, old orange trees give sedate colour to formal city squares. In Japan, koi in shades of orange glide in classic oriental gardens, a cultivated ornament associated with a cultured civilisation.

Like the sun, these colours evoke images of life, and when their tones are interplayed like rays of light they can become a designer's delight.

purple

Long before I understood the sensuality of the colour purple, our greatest poets had been using its evocative imagery. Shakespeare in *A Midsummer Night's Dream* identifies the colour purple with falling in love, for he saw where Cupid's bolt fell:

Before milk-white, now purple with love's wound,
And maidens call it Love-in-idleness.

Many lovers of violets (which are what love-in-idleness is) are oblivious of the fact that this spreading plant is one of the garden's most tolerant ground covers, performing happily in the gloomiest places. I am convinced that every sad suburban front lawn should either become a violet patch, providing a deep mat of leaves and late, late winter flowers, or explode in February with tiny bulbs to unfold as a coverlet of late-winter petals – perhaps the exquisitely purple-striped *Crocus vernus* 'Striped Beauty' or doge-purple *C. v.* 'Remembrance' in abandoned groups that would turn this seasonally neglected garden space into a month of total glamour.

Crocuses are the perfect flowers, for they can be heeled in lightly and forgotten until their reappearance as bright lights on the greyest days, then simply mown down with the first seasonal lawn cut.

Purple flecked through with gold is astonishingly effective. The cool, pale days of spring can be enriched by splashes of an imperial-purple tulip 'Blue Diamond', a strong peony-style flower that sturdily resists prevailing winds. I sometimes plant this mauve tulip with *T.* 'Golden Nizza', a butter ball flecked with scarlet, covering their feet with the newly appearing burgundy leaves of *Heuchera* 'Quick Silver' or wisps of purple and bronze fennel. I would then hide the border's edge under the funnel-shaped violet flowers of *Pulmonaria* 'Blue Ensign' in dappled light, or the valiant *Viola* 'Avril Lawson', rich purple and friendly to tough treatment.

As summer approaches, the neon-purple *Salvia nemorosa* 'Ostfriesland' is as lurid and spine-tingling as purple prose – perhaps Lord Byron's stirring description of a triumphant army in overpowering colour:

The Assyrian came down like the wolf on the fold,
And his cohorts were gleaming in purple and gold.

The combination of Allium christophii *and* Astrantia *'Hadspen Blood' weaves shades of ruby and mauve together.*

Geraniums, Allium christophii *and tall rods of* Dictamnus albus purpureus *blend together at West Green House to form banks that gradually turn the border from mauve to purple.*

The glint of polished spears can be in planted sparks of the golden *Kniphofia* 'Star of Baden Baden', with perhaps *Gaillardia aristata* 'Maxima Aurea', more gold, or my favourite, the burnished *Gaillardia* 'Dazzler', a dainty daisy shape that could be a golden shield.

High-summer light has the strength to match aggressive colour. *Lobelia* x *gerardii* 'Vedrariensis' is a superb plant, used at West Green House to encroach into the garden gaps left by the deep lavender *Papaver* 'Lilac Girl', and accompanied by a purple-bronze canna leaf. *Hemerocallis* 'Prairie Blue Eyes' in a dusty purple, with the 90cm (3ft) stiff stalks of *Verbena bonariensis* and ethereal *Linaria purpurea*, makes an ecclesiastical colour procession that seems to wander through a film of purple light.

Terracotta looks arresting alongside purple, a fact that is inescapable in southern France, so try Mediterranean colour in seasonal pottery pots with deep purple *Agapanthus* 'Purple Cloud', 1.5m (5ft) tall with bright green strappy leaves, above a cascade of blue prostrate rosemary, perhaps *R.* 'Rampant Boule' to make the thickest curtain. Place this pot where there is protection, for this particular agapanthus needs nurturing.

Pots of mauve-purple star-studded balls of *Allium* 'Globemaster' can rise above tumbling clouds of grey-leafed, lavender-flowered *Nepeta* 'Six Hills Giant' that will veil the alliums' feet and stems; for the allium leaves are spent long before it has completed its June flowering, while the sun-loving nepeta will billow from Ali Baba jars until the first cool days of September.

In the potager, purple fruit, flowers, herbs and vegetables enliven rows of green from spring's earliest days. Purple asparagus rises from deeply manured beds contained in bed boxes of purple boards. A dwarf bean 'Dragon Tongue', wax yellow streaked with brilliant purple, looks fun planted in rows between purple wooden tripods hung with the flat pods of the climbing bean 'Purple King' and the purple-magenta sweet pea, *Lathyrus odoratus* 'Matucana'.

An entire vegetable garden can be walled with espaliered deep purple plums like the vegetable maze at the Priory Notre-Dame d'Orsan in France; and trellised walls of cascading purple grapes take us back to gardens in ancient history.

Purple-brown figs will ripen more quickly espaliered to walls, and the aubergines – purple-speckled 'Listada de Gandia' and 'Long White' – dependent on a hot summer and arising above purple annual verbena, another sun-worshipper, provide rich vibrant colour.

Huckleberries, darkly luscious, are autumn delights. I've planted them near compact domes of *Aster novi-belgii* 'Purple Dome' for more saturated late colour, outlined in ruffled purple basil. Opposite, wide bands of purple sage make horizontal ribbons beside the deep shiny-leaved *Dahlia* 'Poem', a sunset orange, forming a subtle play of dull and polished leaves.

These leaves are the colour of shadows. They highlight the brilliant golden tangerine star-shaped flowers that shoot up from this vault of purple in a last splash of colour before the garden falls into its winter slumber; in the words of the song 'Deep Purple':

When the deep purple falls over sleepy garden walls
And the stars begin to flicker in the sky…

The urban eye becomes mono-chromatic, attuned to every shade of grey, the colours of dust and the ever-prevailing black – the consuming colours of Central Business District landscapes. The man-made world of glass, concrete and steel, which we have latterly taken to become city style, has infiltrated from office to drawing room and on to the patio and garden.

On a very special never-to-be-forgotten evening in Paris my impression was one of black light. The long glass doors opened on to a garden

I turned my head from this picture of polished civilisation back to the white and gold room and realised that every woman was in black, with light captured in subdued gems from the old crystal chandeliers. I wondered who else had noticed that the garden, room and people reflected the same stark style and colour.

In subtle variations this is repeated internationally. The interiors of smart shops and restaurants that shine from magazines all seem to have polished cold chrome chairs upholstered in

garden design in the city

and terrace, to an ever-expanding square of raked bands of black and white gravel that formed a courtyard pattern, meeting at right angles a long canal of dark still water. This pure black mirror surface coaxed the eye to a distant *belle époque* fountain, dripping pinpoints of jet-black water. Squares of trim box around clipped trees in Versailles planters stretched out on either side. Sparse old tree branches protected this area from any intrusive neighbouring night colour and ensured a design of arresting simplicity that by night was just a monochrome of shining black and light.

black leather, blond wooden floors and banquettes, and enormous glass vases at the entrance filled with architectural leaves or solo choices of fashionable white arum lilies, luxury orchids or stiff-pointed white florist's roses.

I found I had absorbed this pared-down colour and unconsciously had transferred my urban colour eye to my terrace garden in Sydney. For many of us a city garden will be a balcony or at best a courtyard or terrace, used as an extension of our everyday life, another room open to the sky.

Many of the 'new world' cities hug the coastline – San Francisco, Sydney,

Hong Kong, the hills of Cape Town and Auckland – with housing jostling for a glimpse of sunlit harbours below, and cantilevered terraces and balconies embracing total skylines. This is in complete contrast to northern European urban living: here so often all dwellings are boxed by streets and walls that offer streetscapes and skies that for many months are tonal shades of grey.

The Sydney harbour suburbs are a combination of sand, grey and blue, for they are surrounded by sky and sea, then the cream of sand and the native sandstone, with the dark profiles of the bridge and city skyline on the horizon. We shelter from this brightness in the percolated grey-green shade of eucalyptus trees and

Replicas of ammonites cast in earth tones make smart patterns for paths and terraces that need to be beautiful constructions in their own right.

RIGHT *Grey slate smartly cut and laid epitomises refined urban style. Here slate broken beneath reflecting water emphasises the simplicity of the larger pieces.*

OPPOSITE *Stone steps break a chic repeating pattern in slate.*

discuss what will grow in this nearly subtropical climate.

Sand, white, black and splashes of blue – these Sydney colours were the unthinking hues I used in my city garden, a garden of pots and two small beds. The beige in the marble and sandstone floor of the sitting room and terrace was repeated in Haddonstone pots, benches and a pergola with pillars that supported a white *Wisteria floribunda* 'Alba'.

Height came from poodle-clipped white oleanders, totally unkillable here, and similarly clipped native lilly-pillies – *Syzygium* with black purple leaves shaded green, and dull magenta fruit, an excellent look that became a practical disaster as the falling fruit stained the floor. The replacement was clipped *Cupressus torulosa* that made

plain green practical good sense in this climate, alongside large low-growing white azaleas, 'Alba Magna', and *Gardenia augusta* 'Grandiflora', trusted Sydney stalwarts that added mass to the pots, both as spreading small shrubs and as topiaried standards. Smaller tubs used *Scabiosa caucasica*, a heat-tolerant grey plant with faded French-blue flowers, as a frill around clipped balls of *Teucrium fruticans* in exactly the same hues, adding further rounded shape.

In the two beds, *Datura suaveolens* drooped under pendulous fragrant white trumpets, with spring freesia and summer-flowering Asiatic lily bulbs at its feet; the kitchen parsley formed a green lace border.

High on the retaining walls, the expected classical ornament was replaced by copious pots of the leathery green leaves of agave, a skyline sculpture that never needed any attention. Black came with the balcony railings, iron furniture and the fruit bats that flew at dusk from the Morton Bay fig at the water's edge.

It was a local pastiche of plants, with restrained colour in cream, white and black plus the native palette of all shades of grey and blue.

In a newly renovated London terrace, the basic colours appeared again. The camel-coloured drawing-room carpet was nearly the size of the garden beyond, where the centre of

the courtyard was an oblong of black slate bordered with a band of reproduction stone-coloured fossilised ammonites, utterly smart, with faux Bath stone to the perimeters. Elongated sandstone cream pots held the most eclectic collection of clipped trees, snipped into every possible shape and height, in yew, *Taxus baccata*; box, *Buxus sempervirens* 'Suffruticosa'; and holly, *Ilex aquifolium* 'J.C.Van Tol'.

This geometry was broken on each side by one cascade of *Hydrangea paniculata* 'White Moth' falling from rectangular pots that were placed around the walls. They encircled the paving except where a glass screen, heavily textured like the mark of waves in the sand, shone through a sheet of running water, forming a fountain that provided animated brightness year

round. *Hydrangea petiolaris* attached to horizontal wires covered what remained of the walls behind the pots and glass water sculpture, its seasonal green a soft background foil, its summer flowers softly white.

For most of the year the central glass table became the flower garden. A decorative Mexican tin tray held a capricious collection of earth-coloured pots planted with the regular rosettes of grey sempervivums, spring bulbs and culinary herbs in season – all choices that can be easily maintained. This London garden was half a world away from Sydney but it was another subconscious choosing of 21st-century professional colour, though with a change of greens, now the darkest greens, the lights of now illuminated glass.

To those of us who have always enjoyed gardens of light and colour, a little voice says somewhere, 'Perhaps it's time to do something about it.' Municipal authorities still plant out bright bedding schemes annually in public spaces, but even these massed displays look merely brave, for they do not seem to have any relationship to the size, colour and scope of the city's architecture.

Architects include installations of brightly painted walls, gates and modern sculptures in prestigious developments that are engaging when

new, but the colour unfortunately fades or is defaced before the authorities budget for redecoration. So are these attempts at urban colour harmonious or are they embarrassing? If the latter, do we therefore concede that plants or gardens with form rather than colour are more relevant to the urban environment?

In many mid-western American cities, plantings of native grasses now fill civic gardens and freeway roundabouts, where they are hugely effective in softening the surrounding surfaces. In prairie colours of dull green, brown and wheaten and grey shades they are grown in monumental groups, huge and confident until toppled by snow, reflecting modern architectural colour and brute form in their massed planting. Their texture makes a graceful contrast to the industrial surfaces and the cars clogging the highways.

Already a selection of tough plants that overwinter in Sydney – slender black bamboo *Phyllostachys nigra*, the giant fern fronds of cyclades, the spiked rosettes of glaucous grey agaves – are among the major players in the emerging list of architectural plants that break severe minimalist lines. Used as living sculptures, hardy and perennial, they seem to have become inevitable components of contemporary design.

LEFT Phormium *'Rainbow Sunrise'* and *(right)* Phyllostachys bambusoides *'Castilonis' are both plants of slender lines whose shape and colours provide vertical architecture.*

Into these graphic forms I'd like to introduce some suggestion of the seasons, with plants that can be used in more temperate climates, that are not just colour selections like a pot of petunias; plants from the herbaceous border, the skeletal plants, whose contoured shapes become reflecting shadows on bare walls, bringing a play of light and movement to what are static gardens designed for all seasons.

From tubs with a silvered metal patina I'd introduce the pale silver of cardoons, *Cynara cardunculus*, often 3.6m (12ft) of stark grey scaffolding with spiky leaves, followed by big

Plants with strong shape: top to bottom
Cordyline australis, Agave parryi *and*
Miscanthus sinensis *'Zebrinus'*.

purple thistle flower heads, in leaf from early spring into the autumn, when they can be cut back and the pot removed.

Into this grouping I'd place more French-blue thistles, growing from artichokes, which have leaves of acanthus style and consequence. In warm climates the leaves die back; however, they regenerate immediately and remain until the frosts.

Eryngium agavifolium would continue the thistle form with cones of silvered green on spindle stems, together with *Echinops ritro*, a tough, very ordinary plant that is tall and straight, so that when controlled within a square container it makes a geometric oblong that could be likened to a super-size bin of marshalled bright blue drumsticks.

Another arresting plant is the yellow and green striped grass *Miscanthus sinensis* 'Zebrinus', a 1.8m (6ft) giant that also grows straight and tall, handsomely marked with zebra bands of yellow. Again, it can form tall, oblong columns rising from geometrically shaped planters.

Urban space dictates that many of these gardens are enclosed and restricted by surrounding walls, a necessity that creates one of the most perfect environments for aromatic plants, for tall walls capture any heat, which intensifies the fragrance of the plants within their confines.

Among the clipped shrubs and trees in proven evergreen box, holly and yew that are now *de rigueur*, a few well-shaped evergreen flowering shrubs can provide an oasis of compelling fragrance, perhaps a form of aromatherapy for the exhausted city dweller.

Always handsome, and smothered in pure white, sweetly perfumed waxy flowers in late spring, the Mexican orange blossom, *Choisya ternata*, has polished green leaves. *Elaeagnus ebbingei* is a neat shrub with an insignificant greenish flower of delicious fragrance. Both would make excellent complements to the precisely clipped shapes, their perfume intriguing enough to add spice to the minimalist garden.

Although slow to establish, evergreen *Osmanthus delavayi* has highly fragrant white tubular flowers, and *O. ledifolius* becomes clustered stars smelling of honey. Compact, slow-growing – and, thankfully, they both rather like being left alone by clipping shears – they will form, with very little help, deliciously fragrant garden shape.

The warm courtyard is the ideal environment for the statuesque *Magnolia grandiflora,* with khaki reverse leaves, which can be clipped into free-form pyramids of noble proportions. For this tree can reach the eaves of a two-storey house. Magnificent either as a single plant or in regimented lines, it bears its flowers singly, giving a day of pure cream spectacle and hypnotic fragrance. A courtyard decorated with these plants alone in fine containers is cultured style for me.

The tiny blossom of lemons exudes the most spicy of perfumes. For those with the climate to grow these trees, this is another plant to consider. Smartly trimmed in pots, set out in an entire garden as a parade-ground grid with their trunks painted white, they are reminiscent of Renaissance style so elegant that it cannot be superseded.

The rampant jasmine *Jasminum polyanthum* is for warmer climates. Its white to pink flowers simply overpower on spring evenings and it quickly covers walls, making it an excellent screen for unwanted views. If chocolate is a secret vice, *Akebia quinata* will entice with its chocolate spice perfume. This climber, also known as the chocolate vine, needs a warm enclosed courtyard, where it will quickly smother its support to bloom with a deep pink-brown flower in spring followed, if the summer is long and hot, with a sausage-shaped purple fruit. Plant two together to ensure fruiting.

Encompassing buildings can create dense pools of deep shade or, conversely, sun-traps, both of which are anathema to conventional lawns, so paving opens up many intriguing prospects for city gardens.

I like floorings that are bold all-weather grids, perhaps formal squares of dark slate broken by pale marble lines, or sets of faux cobblestones crossed by strong bands of terracotta tiles.

A pale sandstone paving was broken by a grid of glass tiles that became lit graph paper by night, and a rustic flooring of coarse wooden railway sleepers was lightened by their being placed about 12.5cm (5in) apart and the gap being filled with cream pebbles. Remember that treated timber decking slats, although a very appealing surface, do become very slippery in wet weather, as do many tile surfaces.

In an all-over paving of stone blocks, bricks or tiles, a hard landscape mat constructed from mosaics in tiles or coloured pebbles can enliven the principal sitting area, but I'd still choose colours that were muted and sophisticated, and attuned to the metropolis.

As I live with gardens that seem to have many gravel paths, and as each morning I spend time sweeping out endless tiny stones, I'm not sure I'd choose to surface a space very close to the house with gravel again. But I remember the disco floors of my youth, chequerboards of bright light, and say, why not a pulsating patio of colour?

The surrounding walls and fences in our urban gardens are all-pervasive, so their surfaces by default become a major feature of the garden. Perhaps the walls of an urban garden are the place to introduce colour. Deep Pompeii red would highlight a line of light-coloured urns or a tall spiky row of creamy yucca bells.

The colour of storm clouds, navy-grey with a hint of green, marketed as 'Thunderclap', is a powerful backdrop for terracotta and sandstone. In fact I find it the most sympathetic garden colour, atmospheric but strong, exceptional for garden furniture.

Consider the deepest sienna broken by mounds of tidy green *Skimmia* 'Bronze Knight', with deep brown flower buds, or a deep Mediterranean-blue wall with frontal rods of yellow kniphofias, or forsythia, one of the earliest golden yellow flowers to cover bare branches.

If light allows, my first thoughts always turn to espalier designs using all manner of trees, the branches attached to wires to make the patterns. The bronze winter leaves of beech trees look superb against pale walls, as do the traditional golden laburnums would light a wall for one exceptional week each year. Floodlit from path lights beneath, the trees can create linear tracery either from a line of floor spotlights or from a strip of light.

The urban garden is so often another sitting room, used and viewed at night, so lighting effects make another arena.

Lit water can be as curtains falling over river pebbles, or a series of single water jets, shooting to varying heights from a floor-lit paving grid. Water backed by a dark mirror has double the impact, capturing both sun and night light. *Amelanchier lamarckii*, a tree for all seasons, encased in white spring flowers and pulsating with flame-coloured leaves by autumn, and snaking rivers of optic light are perpetual choices.

So perhaps we have to come to accept that where we plan a city garden, we jettison our preconceived ideas of gardening, considering only the tones and shapes around us, and

Controlled and elegant use of water, trees and clipped formality in an urban courtyard designed by George Carter.

reflecting in our choice of plants and hard-landscaping surfaces what looks harmonious outside the glass. Perhaps we have to accept that there is a time when we do settle for smart minimal colour and design, in which case, let's play with only shape, texture and light, choosing plants that can withstand an environment of heavy pollution, shade pockets and wind tunnels, just as we do when adapting to such elements in other extreme gardening environments.

index

Acer negundo 'Flamingo' 30
Acer palmatum 53, 93
Achillea 20, 73, 76, 167
Aconitum 162
Actea 104
Akebia quinata 188
Alhambra Palace 66
Allium 'Globe Master' 51, 177
Annuals 120-129
Aquilegia 104, 115, 168
Architecture and art, fusing 44
Artemisia 162
Aruncus dioicus 55
Astilbe chinensis 'Veronica Klose' 54
Astrantia major 'Celtic Star' 51
Australia, gardens in 11, 13
Azaleas 181

Beachside plantings 124, 127
Beech, copper 30
Benches 81, 82
Berberis thunbergii 53
Bluebells 156-159
Border edges 132
Box 34, 183
  see also *Buxus*
British colonists' gardens 8, 11
Briza maxima 127
Brown plants 164, 167
Brussels sprouts 156
Buddleia 96
Bunya Bunya pine 11
Buskers End 92
Buxus sempervirens 'Suffruticosa' 14

Cabbages 156
Calendula 164
Camellia sasanqua 60

Carex flagellifera 92
Carter, George 17
Carvallo, Dr 17
Catmint 70
Cerinthe major 124
Chewter, Mike 78
Choisya ternata 187
Christopher, Marina 115, 164
Cirsium 115, 116
Cistus 98
Citrus colours 170-173
Citrus trees 68
City, garden design in 178-189
Clematis 48, 76, 117, 118
Climate, plants suitable for 37, 38
Climate variations 58
Coastline cities 179
Colonnades 149
Colour, designing with 160-177
Compost heaps 131
Compton, Jamie 115
Convallaria 51
Cook, Michael 42
Cooking, planting for 132, 133
Corn 134
Cornus alba 'Sibirica' 86
Cornus controversa 'Variegata' 50
Cornus kousa 51, 53
Cosmos bipinnatus 'Purity' 123
Cotinus coggygria 58
Cotoneaster 98
Cottage garden 11 romantic 110-113
Cow parsley 115
Crambe cordifolia 116
Crocuses 174
Cupressus torulosa 181
Cut-out figures 81
Cyclamen 93
Cynara cardunculus 184

Daffodils 156-159
Dahlias 63, 102, 104
Datura suaveolens 181
Decoration 80-83

Deschampsia cespitosa 'Bronzeschleier' 55
Designers 36
Dianthus 168
Diascia 123
Digitalis 164, 167
Dunn, Douglas 38

Earth and oil colours 164-168
Eastern architecture, use of 40
Echium 162
Echinops 162
Elderflower hedge 85
Eleagnus ebbingei 187
Enclosed gardens 66
Entrances 83
Epimedium x *versicolor* 'Sulphureum' 51
Eryngium 162
Espaliered trees 30
Eucalyptus 86, 180
Euphorbia 123

Festuca glauca 'Blaufuchs' 17
Formal gardens 61
Frame, pattern needing 29
Fritillaria 164
Fruit 76, 177

Garden rhythm 48-57
Garden style 22-39
Gardening advice 36
Geometric shapes 57
Geranium pratense 'Victor Reiter Junior' 51
Geranium wallichianum 'Buxton's Variety' 113
Giardini della Landriana 146, 160
Gourds 123
Grasses 116, 183
Green architecture 62
Grey gardens 42
Grey plants 160-162
Gypsophila 116

Hakea 60
Hard landscaping 36, 37, 57, 61-63

Hazeley Court 17
Hedges 14
Hemerocallis 'American Revolution' 21
Herb garden 138-143
Herbs 70, 130
Hinkley, Dan 42
Hobhouse, Penelope 67
Hollyhocks 127, 164
Honeysuckle 113
Hosta 162, 172
Humulus lupulus 'Aureus' 117
Hydrangeas 94, 95
Hypericum calycinum 20

Ilex 95, 183
Inspiration for design 16-18
Iris 156-159
Iris 'Pacific Mist' 93
Iris 'Titan Glory' 51
Iris sibirica 138, 158
Iris germanica 14, 51, 162

Jasmine 187
Jekyll, Gertrude 11

Kale 156
Kiley, Dan 65
Kniphofia 'Nancy's Red' 53
Kumquats 113

Lancaster, Nancy 17
Landscape, colour wash of 42
Larkspur 162
Lattice pyramid 33
Lavender 70, 72, 73, 113
Layers, garden in 60
Leaf vegetables 133, 137
Lemons 187
Lennox-Boyd, Arabella 17, 29
Lettuce 133
Leylandii cypresses 14
Likkierman, Michael 64
Lilac 113
Linear design 33
Lobelia 62, 76, 124
Local gardens, ideas from 58

Low-maintenance gardening 59
Lutyens, Sir Edwin 11

Magnolia 170, 187
Mahonia 99
Malus floribunda 61
Mapperton 21
Martagon lilies 159
Meadow flowers 123
Meadow garden 85, 106, 108
Miscanthus sinensis 27, 161, 187
Mogul garden 66-78
Monkey puzzle 11
Mortola, La 18
Movement, plants with 54, 55
Myrtus apiculata 20

Nasturtium 124
Native American garden 134-136
Native plants, using 43
New World cities 179
Norfolk Island pine 11
Nyssa sylvatica 48

Objects, use of 80-83
Oleanders 180
Oriental vegetable garden 136-138
Osmanthus delavayi 187
Osteospermum 127

Pagan, Sir Jock and Lady 8
Page, Russell 17, 146, 160
Painted supports 148
Pansies 70
Peonies 102
Peppers 133, 134
Persian carpet designs 70, 72
Persona, garden 40-47
Pests 132, 162
Phaseolus caracalla 117
Philadelphus 94
Plane tree 91
Plant supports 132
Planting design 20, 21
Pleached trees 30, 31, 61
Poppies 102
Potager 132, 133

Pots, vegetables and herbs in 130
Practical gardens 60
Provence 29, 42
Prunus serrula 'Miyako' 164
Prunus 'Ukon' 92
Purple plants 174-177
Pyracantha 98
Pyrus salicifolia 'Pendula' 188

Quest-Ritson, Charles 162

Ratatouille 133
Ricinus communis 'Carmencita' 123
Robinson, William 11
Rodgersia 55
Romantic gardens 101-113
Roses 70, 72, 78
  arch, covering 49
  climbing 117, 118
  designing with 145-151
  fragrant garden 151
  Giardini della Landriana 146
  grey 162
  heritage 151, 152
  Nimfa, at 147
  traditional garden 145
  trusses, on 147, 148
  varieties 151, 152

Salvia 73
Sambucus nigra 51, 85
Scabiosa caucasica 181
Scheherezade's paradise 66-78
Schwartz, Martha 17, 22, 23, 29, 64
Seasons 14
Sedum 'Autumn Joy' 27
Setaria 'Lowlander' 92
Shrubs
  groups, in 99
  parterres 95
  planting 94-99
  serpentine border 94
Skimmia 'Brown Knight' 188
Silex caprea 'Kilmarnock' 93
Single plant, designing with 145-159

Sissinghurst Castle 17
Sisyrinchium striatum 'Variegatum' 51
Sorbus aria 'Lutescens' 30
St Jean de Beauregard 127
Starting from scratch 58-65
Statues 80
Stipa gigantea 117
Stipa tenuissima 55
Stone walls 61
Strong colour, patterns of 53
Sweden, James van 27
Sweet peas 123, 168
Swiss chard 157
Sydney harbour 179
Syringa vulgaris 'Katherine Hevemeyer' 113
Syzygium 180

Tapestry hedge 30
Taverna, Lavinia 146
Tellima grandiflora Rubra Group 52
Terrace, paved 59, 62, 63
Teucrium fruticans 181
Thalictrum 116
Tiarella 52
Tomatoes 133, 134
Topiary 30, 33-35
Trees
  choice of 89
  citrus 68
  colours 93
  designing with 86, 88
  espaliered 30
  green 30
  ground under 92
  height, bringing to garden 31
  leaf, size of 91
  naturalising 86-93
  planting 91
  pleached 30, 31, 61
  practicalities 89-91
  seat round 92
  tracery designs, inspiration for 42
  tropical 42
  water, need for 90
  woodland glade 86

Tripods, grouping 33
Tropaeolum 117
Tulips 33, 115, 154-156

Umbellifer family 115
Urbanisation 43, 44

Valder, Dr Peter 119
Vegetable gardens 130-143
Veiled plants 115-119
Verbena 73, 124
Verbascum 164
Versailles 173
Vesian, Nicole de 29, 160
Viburnum 51
Villandry, Château de 17
Vines 48, 117, 132
Violas 70, 123
Violets 174

Walling, Edna 11
Water
  flowing 54
  formal Italian garden 77
  irrigated 68
  islands 78
  lit 188
  rills, grid design 67
  romantic garden, in 104, 105
  use of 64, 65
Water lilies 65
Weigela 96
Whatley Manor 63
Wisteria 119, 180

Yew 34, 183

Zinnias 72, 124

Marylyn Abbott would like to thank:

Rosemary Alexander, James van Sweden, Charles Quest-Ritson, Guy Cooper and Gordon Taylor for introductions to plants and gardens

Lucinda and Carolo Lequio di Assaba, who gave me their atelier in Verona, Italy, to write in.

Photographic acknowledgements

SG = Simon Griffiths
CP = Clay Perry
AL = Andrew Lawson
JH = Jerry Harpur
MH = Marcus Harpur
NB = Nicola Browne
JG = John Glover
GPL = Garden Picture Library

p. 1 SG; pp. 2/3 CP; pp. 4/5 AL; p. 6 CP; pp. 6/7, 9 SG; p. 10 Michael Bligh & Associates, Landscape Architects, website: www.michaelbligh.com.au; p. 12 JH (Cruden Farm, Victoria, Australia); p. 15 CP; p. 16 Bridgeman Art Library/Chateau de Versailles, France, photograph by Peter Willi; pp. 18/19 JH (RHS Chelsea 1998, Evening Standard Garden, design Arabella Lennox-Boyd); pp. 20/21 NB; pp. 22/23 NB (design Martha Schartz, New Mexico); pp. 23, 24/25 (both pictures) JH (design Martha Schwartz; Sam & Anne Davies' garden, El Paso, Texas); pp. 26/27 AL (design Oehme &

2004, design Jane Hudson & Erik de Maeiter); pp. 58/59 CP; pp. 60/61 JH (Titoke Point, New Zealand); pp. 62/63 JH (Arabella Lennox-Boyd, Gresgarth Hall); p. 64 JH (Sir Richard Carew Pole, Antony, Cornwall); pp. 67, 68/69 Coty Farquhar; p. 72 SG; pp. 73, 74/75, 78 CP; pp. 80/81 Coty Farquhar; p. 82 SG; pp. 83, 84 CP; pp. 84/85 AL (design Piet Oudolf, Hummelo); pp. 86/87 SG; p. 88/89 CP; pp. 90/91 NB (design Laure Quonium, Ile-de-France); p. 93 Clive Nicholls; pp. 94/95 JG; pp 96, 97 (left & right) AL; p. 97 centre JG; pp. 98, 99 CP; p. 100 SG; pp. 102/103 (all pictures) Claire Austin; p. 105 (both pictures) SG; p. 106 JH (design Helen Dillon, Dublin); pp. 106/107 AL (design Helen Dillon, Dublin); p. 108 JH (design Dan Kiley; Kimmel residence, Connecticut); p. 109 AL (design Arabella Lennox-Boyd, Gresgarth Hall); pp. 110/111 JH (design Arabella Lennox-Boyd, Gresgarth Hall); pp. 112, 114/115, 116/117 AL; p. 118/119 Peter Valder; pp. 120/121, 122, 125 (both pictures), 126/127 CP, 128/129, 130/131, 133 CP; p. 134 Clive Boursnell; p. 139 Bridgeman Art Library/Victoria & Albert

acknowledgements

Pepe Hudson, Julie Bostock, Christine Bugg, Danussa Rogowska and Louise Pialek for practical assistance; Paul Welti for fine design; and editor Caroline Taggart, a lady of exceptional patience.

And as ever, the West Green House gardeners, who create the superb displays each spring, and my cousin Bill Gray, who has started a new career as a gardener, supervising the gardens at Kennerton Green.

van Sweden); p. 27 JH (design Oehme & van Sweden); pp. 28/29 (both pictures) Vivien Russell (design the late Nicole de Vesian); pp. 30/31 JH (design Michael Balston & Arabella Lennox-Boyd, Little Malvern Court); p. 32 (both pictures) CP; p. 33 JG (willow pyramid by Barbara Hunt); p. 34 NB (design Kathryn Gustafson, Terrasson, France); p. 35 left AL (Rodmarton Manor, Gloucestershire); p. 35 right JG (design Jonathan Baillie); pp. 36/37 SG; pp. 38/39 GPL/John Glover (RHS Chelsea 2000, design Tom Stuart-Smith); p. 41 Bridgeman Art Library/Archive Charmet (seventeenth-century Chinese, colour on silk); p. 43 CP (RHS Chelsea 2004, design Nicholas Tripp Associates); pp. 44/45 Russell Johnson (Dale Chihuly, Niijima Float installation, 1992, Honolulu, Hawaii); p. 46 Terry Rishel (Dale Chihuly, Niijima Floats, 2001, Chicago, Illinois); p. 47 Terry Rishel (Dale Chihuly, Persian Pond, 2001, Chicago, Illinois); pp. 48/49 SG; p. 50 Le Scanff/ Mayer; p. 52 NB (RHS Chelsea, design Andy Sturgeon); p. 53 JH (design Jack Lenor Larsen, Long House Reserve, USA); p. 54 MH (design Jorn Langberg, Suffolk); p. 55 (both pictures) CP (RHS Chelsea, 2004, design Nicholas Tripp Associates); pp. 56/57 AL (RHS Chelsea

Museum, London (from the memoirs of Babur, Mughal, 1589–90); pp. 142/143 (all pictures), 144 CP; p. 147 AL; p. 148 NB (design Kathryn Gustafson, Terrasson, France); pp. 149, 150 left & right AL; p. 150 centre JG; pp. 152/153, 154, 156/157 CP; p. 158 CP (Bunny Guinness, RHS Chelsea 2004); p. 159 AL (RHS Chelsesa 2004, design Bunny Guinness); pp. 160/161 SG; p. 163 (all pictures) AL; p. 165 CP; p. 166 MH (Harvey's Garden Plants, Bradfield, Suffolk); p. 167 GPL/Clive Nicholls (Hadspen Garden); p. 169 left AL; p. 169 right CP; pp. 170/171, 172 NB (both design Dan Pearson, Home Farm, Hampshire); p. 173 JG; pp. 174/75, 176 CP; p. 178/9 MH (Great Glemham House, Suffolk); p. 180 AL (design Patrick Wynniatt-Husey & Patrick Clarke); p. 181 JH (design Robert Chittock, Seattle, Washington); p. 182 left AL; p. 182 centre MH (Great Glemham House, Suffolk); p. 182 right MH (RHS Chelsea 2002, design David Rosewarne & Magie Gray); p. 184 JG; p. 185 AL; p. 186 top MH; p. 186 centre JH; p. 186 bottom MH (Harvey's Garden Plants, Bradfield St George, Suffolk); p. 189 Marianne Majerus (RHS Chelsea 1999, The Christie Sculpture Garden, design George Carter)